The Libyan Years

San Daniel

Published by San Daniel, 2021.

While every precaution has been taken in the preparation of this book, the publisher assumes no responsibility for errors or omissions, or for damages resulting from the use of the information contained herein.

The Libyan Years

Previously published under: 1680902644, 978-1680902648

Second edition. November 22, 2021.

Copyright © 2021 San Daniel.

Written by San Daniel.

The Libyan Years

The seven day war

The seven-day war was fought between 5 and June 10, 1967, between Israel and Syria, Egypt and Jordan. The war is also known as the Six Day War. The real official hostilities lasted 5 days but in reality, the area was and had been a hotbed of unrest. The skirmishes and provocations were much longer in place. Egypt at that time had Abdhul Nasser as president, who was seen as the big man in the Arab world.

At that time, our family lived in Lybia, the neighboring country of Egypt. For months it was brewing, even in Libya where we lived. My father worked at the Oasis oil company an American conglomerate that held many concessions in the desert. We had lived there for many years. My father was one of the oil boys, a group of experts who realized Texan turnkey projects all over the world. The client orders the construction of refineries and crackers, wells and so forth and they only need to turn the key to start the process, hence turnkey projects. They were men with a heavy technical training and a lot of oil experience. My father and I were so similar in name and being that we could not pass through one door for years, 40 years, to be precise. Highly individualistic, you might say.

My dad always worked on four year contracts, then the whole *rasmedan* was operational, there was one year a trial run, the fifth year, which was meant to perform, if necessary, troubleshooting and to proceed to a seamless transfer. You are talking about millions and millions dollar projects. So we lived every 5 years again in another country. It has its drawbacks but on the other hand, you develop a different perspective on the world.

In Libya, the division between rich and poor natives is very big one. Russia, and I would actually have to speak of, at that time, the Soviet Union, always fi red the Arab countries up against the Western world and most Arabs saw the Americans and everything associated with it, as devils and the Russians as the friends of the Utopia state that 'helped' them. It was non existing aid from the Soviets. They seized the Palestinian issue eagerly to project America as pro-Israel and therefore anti-Arab, which was not so and so to drive a wedge

6in a mock war that would later be called. the cold war. The Cold War was not only a field of tension in Europe, but it also included the Arab world.

They were pawns in these conflicts for only one reason, oil. My father, who was born in Indonesia as a Dutch colonist, had a keen eye for negative developments, political developments and threatening developments and could evaluate the time we lived in well. He was a man with a strong survival instinct and is one of the most intelligent people I have ever met in my life. The civilized world still came by, from the slaughter parties in the Belgian Congo, and the Japanese attack on Singapore and Indonesia only a few years before, coupled to all the atrocities of actions directed against the white people, and it hung like a warning cloud over the heads of the non-arab whites who worked in the oil countries.

Racial hatred is bad and if times deteriorate, than hate thickens like molasses in the sky, you feel where you walk as a white minority that hate, the intense hatred, every day. You feel the eyes in your back and you keep your back straight, because if you show fear, the others feel that, and a stone is easily picked up and thrown. Unfortunately, in these sort of countries, if someone throws a stone, it seems to work very contagious and in no time everyone throws stones. If you do not have a shelter, they'll stone you to death. Just like that. Because you're white, or because they think you are American, or Christian. Or just because they can do it. Or because of the envy or the frustrations they feel and can give no direction to.

The Americans had the technology and the resources and Lybia had plenty of oil and was a backwater. It started a few months before June 5, 1967, the only tv station that Libya was rich, thanks to the Americans, incidentally, blurred hourly military marches out, followed by bombastic nationalist bluster of Nasser. The only newspaper that we were rich was nationalized, that's a sign on the wall. It then became a mouthpiece of politicians. A newspaper such as the Sunday *Chibli* (the Sunday sandstorm), only carried articles now, praising the USSR, it was all about Soviet Russia and the blessings of her five years plans. The evils of capitalism and many insinuations towards American Gringo's whose sole purpose seemed to be to do away with all the Arabs and hand their countries over to Israel.

King Idris at that time was 78 years old and half senile and still a feudal ruler over Libya, he joined in to support his Arabic comrades who "suffered" so much from the Americans and its vassal state of Israel. Everyone forgot that the American companies were the only real major employers in Libya and much wealth was brought by her technique to a country which consisted of backward, illiterate goat milkers, who easily could be manipulated in all directions be it for nationalistic or religious reasons.

For every engineer, every American or European technician, that the oil companies hired, the same number of useless Libyans were taken on. My father could not assign these people to whatever job and all though they were on the payroll, they were a danger in a heavy engineering environment and they were just fine sitting on their bum outside the compounds in the shade. Two completely separate worlds. Which would never quite come together. People who have difficulty calculating, 3 x 3 should be kept away from professional environments where hydrogen gas is separated and stored. Where oil is cracked in complex processes where pressure gauges and readings thereof, determine your life or death.

We saw it coming. Coca Cola was banned by royal decree. Garages that repaired the few American cars, closed. The Dutch consulate left. A week later all American products were boycotted. The hatred shone of the houses and reflected occasionally through the streets and searched for us like an eager bloodthirsty hand. The American channel went off the air. Wheelus Airbase that lay only two kilometers from us, closed its gates. Americans brought their families to the base and the men went back into the desert to work on the technical complexes. We were refused, we had to drive back being non American and in the distance cars were put on their sides, people were pulled out and set on fire. Non Americans were not allowed to enter the base. They stationed a few tanks at the gate, and men with machine-gun post. Wheelus had nuclear weapons on the basis and at that the time was a springboard for the entire Middle East.

Wheelus had been well informed, it was not until several weeks later, that the real conflict broke out. My mother asked me to buy a loaf of bread at the bakery on the corner of the street. My mother and my sisters were never on the street because they'd be harassed immediately, women belong home and not alone on a street. Someone walked up behind me, who started screaming fi rst softly, then louder and louder. A stone flew through the air. I did not look, but walked with a straight back, being the brave little boy that I was.

Now more stones followed, accompanied by more voices and a stone hit my shoulder, I got it, I started to run and as a fury it now rained stones. They were hunting and I was the prey. I looked over my shoulder and saw a familiar face. Among the throwers ran an Arab friend of mine, Abat Mesjier, he had a hand full of stones, and his eyes were wild. I was hit on my head and I felt something warm running in to my neck. Now I ran like a madman. The worst thing was that even adults now were throwing stones, no empathy, no conscience, savages who smell blood. You are obviously very brave when you stone a child to death. There was an Arab man working in his garden and he stepped in front of me, into the street. He started yelling incredibly against the stone throwers and he clenched a fist and folded his cloak around me and carried me in to his garden. Over a path, to his home.

He dabbed the blood away and was very friendly. I thanked him with the little that we spoke Arabic and were obliged to learn at school. *Soekroen ivendi*, Thank you sir. Another man came with a cup Sjahi, a very sweet tea. They were a family that worked for an American company. He spoke broken English and said that I should not be alone the street. "people crazy, for God and Americans". He walked along with me, I bought my loaf of bread and he brought me back to my house. So I've always been helped in my life. I am convinced that if I had not been saved by the energetic Americanized Arab, I would have been stoned to death and they would have left me for the dogs.

I despise with all my heart the cowardly mentality of the stone-throwers and I am the Arab who saved me still very grateful. King Idris had joined the Jihad, the holy war against the pagans. That is what the tea bringing Arabs tried to tell me. **"People crazy, for God and Americans"**

My mother was shocked when she saw me, head wounds always bleed in a very exaggerated way and locked the gates. My father would fly in the next day from the desert. The concessions were 300 kilometers away from Tripoli, and the company used Piper cubs to fly engineers in and out. Now only military march music was being broadcasted, my older brother came home from the College of advanced technology, a British American type Oil college, focused on oil functions. He was upset. The institute was declared undesirable, people were driven out, Arab youth of the better classes shall I say and professors and whites so to speak, and before being sealed an Arabic policeman came out laughing and threw piles of papers into the wind, they blew away slowly.

This was long before the civilized world, but suspected a conflict. It was the build up to the 7 day war. Everything was grim. Stores locked up. Besides, as a white, you could not go into the city. Mohammed our garden boy did the shopping for us.

My father came home and immediately took off the sign Oasis oil company from our home. A plastic shield that was on all the houses of the company, so that the company driver could find employees easier. My father as a technician, was very pragmatic. This I have experienced before, he said. Oasis Oil rang, the fi rm was taken over and had been nationalized and was closed indefinitely. A few Americans decided to leave the neighborhood. Their car was thrown upside down and set on fire the people burned alive.

The radio announced the war and went into a lot of bombastic bluster. Libya sent his air force, starfighters, which they had purchased from the Americans to assist Egypt. Lybia sent troops and all who wanted to fight for Allah, could volunteer. They must have thought that Israel was a pushover. Once and for all Israel would disappear, it would be wiped off the map. People were delirious with lust and war, Nasser was the great man who dared to take on America and Israel The Israelites did not have slow starfighters, they flew in the French Mirages, at that time the most advanced war machine. They were trained in America and the pilots spoke English amongst themselves. The radar of Egypt was focussed on Israel. The Israeli Mirages flew towards Malta, made a slight bend and came attacking Egypt over the 10Libyan side. The side of the ally. They bombed their airport almost entirely before the Egyptian fighters came loose. The few who found the sky were shot out of it.

Egypt had suffered a blow and Libya had lost her complete airforce, The curve that the Mirages had flown and their English conversation, was immediately claimed as proof that the Americans off Wheelus airbase had conducted a cowardly attack and had attacked Egypt in the back. Prestige is in the Arab world an asset and yes, you do want to explain your defeat, ofcourse.. We lived two miles from Wheelus Airbase, believe me, not a single plane had taken off!! The Americans denied an attack, but then they would have done so if they would have attacked. Everyone white or American could now be murdered.

My father grabbed his gun and walked out of the door at to the end of the street and shot a few times in the air and came walking back, in front of our garden, he shot once more in the air. 'So' said the pragmatic father everyone here now knows we have weapons. We went to the table and my father said, find some small things that you are really attached to. If we stay here, we will all be killed, and if not now then a bit later. I wrote a letter to Janet, a girl I knew from school ,and liked a lot and asked Muhammad to post that.

My father went out and cut down the poles of our swing Otherwise they will soon hang us from our own swings he said. My brother and I helped him with that. My brother asked, 'should we get outta here?' 'Certainly', my father said, 'I have experienced this in Indonesia with the KNIL Women are raped and abused and we will be killed and they will mutilate our bodies afterwards to humiliate our race'. 'Oh', we said, startled. My father looked blurry in front of him and said if the stupid masses start moving there is no stopping it. 'But if we are dead what can they can do to us', I asked? 'Boy', my father said, 'you can not imagine how bad man is in time of war'. I have found my friends back in Indonesia, hung with their balls cut off and stuffed in their mouths. We understood it.

He called Muhammad, and gave him a couple of Libyan pounds.' Mohammed,' he said, 'we are going to travel, we will come back, so take good care of our house, I'll pay you more when I get back.' 'Do we come back then,' I asked, surprised? 'If we do not get away',

yes, said my father pragmatically, then 'd like my house not to be ransacked.

A little later we were all in the Opel, tight, really tight altogether. My mother sat next to me in the back with a sister on her lap. My big sister was sitting next to me also with a sister on her lap. Our fate was linked. Here everything could end in a nasty way. My father drove, my brother sat beside him with the shotgun between his legs. We saw some houses nearby on fi re. Thick clouds of smoke drifted over our street. There were many groups on the street. 'Open your window and shoot in the air,' commanded my father, while he was driving to meet the groups head on. My brother obeyed and they scampered away, and we raced right on. I had no idea where my father would go, but my father worked his plan off as he always did, professional, rational and calm, with everything under control. We drove to the old part of Tripoli and I felt panic rising in me, we had to navigate around all kinds of car wrecks that were burnt. Occasionally my brother shot in the air and so we arrived at the port. The barrier stopped us. Two Libyan customs officers came running out. they looked questioningly at my father.

'We have come to say goodbye to friends', my father said as he gave them a bundle of pounds and he pointed to my brother. My brother with the gun. The first man saluted and snarled something to the second one, the barrier went up. We drove along the quay where cranes were unemployed. 'Find a European flag', commanded my father. Moments later we saw a coaster with an Italian flag. My father stopped next to it. 'Out of the car,' my father said, 'you all continue to wait,'. To my brother he said, he I have to arrange something, shoot whatever is not European or American'. My father walked up the ramp and after a time that seemed like an eternity, he came back. 'Go on up,' he said. We walked up the ramp and we saw how my dad just drove the car on a net and how he was hoisted up by a hoisting installation car and all, right on the deck. He got out and said, 'we are now on Italian territory we've done it'. He laughed in a relaxed way.

It must have cost him a few pounds. Moments later, the ropes were cast off and we were carried away from a country that hates everything that is not Arab. My brother had the gun still under his arm. 'Can I see that,' asked my dad and pragmatic as he was with a flourish, he threw it into the sea. In the distance we saw the palms of Libya disappearing along the shoreline until a faint streak remained. A coastline that in my life I would be happy never to see again...A day later, we took our residence in Catanzaro a South Italian place. We had to wait until my dad could get back in touch with his employer and the balances of the bank accounts were no longer frozen. They were wonderful weeks, we could just walk the streets without being hated. It took some weeks, and then my father's affairs were financially sorted out and he took on a contract in Canada,. Alberta to be exact. He had secured an appointment at the University of Calgary and there we went from the heat to the cold and I left for always that wonderful country with that cowardly people behind me.

To the post office

It was a summer day, hot, really hot. You moved as little as possible. My mother had managed to convert a piece of dry land to garden. She was very fond of plants and in beds that she had laid out colored the eastern Indian cherry towards you. That was strange because none of the neighbors had anything that resembled a garden in the slightest. It was warm, the sun burned and singed on your skin. I sat on the steps to the back door, on either side of me a shrubbery of flowers. There was nothing to do. In Libya in the 60s, there was never anything to do. It was holiday time and there was no school. You could not have gone to school because the temperature fluctuated during this time of the year between 40 and 50 degrees Celsius. Even the flies were lazy.

Beyond the shrubberies, my father had made two swings for my kid sisters . I always kept an eye on them as they were playing, you could not leave girls out of sight. Libya is a foreign country concerning girls and women. My father's car was parked at the gate under a huge date tree and a little further was a large empty oil drum where neighbors and we ourselves threw our garbage in. Every second day Mohammed came past, the gardener with a cart, which was pulled by a donkey and he would empty the barrel. Then he disappeared off the yard, taking the smell of rot along. I've never asked myself where he was going with that garbage. It was of no importance, the smell was gone and that was what mattered. Mohammed always had a white fez on his head, which was not something to be laughed at, he had at least once been to Mecca on pilgrimage. There is a gradation in the colors of the fezzes, an Arab neighbor boy had once told me. Reddish purple meant that you had been to Mecca seven times and then you were treated in your environment as a kind of saint. It was a lazy day and the heat just hung in the air and took away any initiative whatsoever. From an unconscious automatism you waved some flies away forever.

My father had a few days off. He had been a few weeks in the desert to the concessions and now he had some free days to settle as compensation for all the suffering there. My father stepped out the door and asked if I wanted to go with him to town. 'Of course,' I said.

14'Where are we going?' 'To the center,' said my father. 'I have to go to the post office, mailbox and go past our office next to the *Souk*.' You could not get to the souk by a car. it was a road that cut through the oldest parts of the center, where every day an Oriental market was held. You parked your car and then you had to continue by foot.

Vegetables and fruits, figs and incredible bags that were half open, with herbs and spices. If you just held in then immediately a market trader was at you and gave you a small glass chai . Sweet strong tea. Out of courtesy you did not, refuse although you could see saw the lip prints from previous customers. Cloths and rags, endless stalls selling carpets and rugs. You walked first among the city gate and then came through an alley-like street with metal workers. Boys who worked copper and figures, hammering them out, templates and hammers. Some of them younger than I was. An already overwhelming buzz accompanied you. At the gate there were always beggars, that was nasty, they mutilated themselves, or used to be maimed by their parents and with a festering wound to an arm or stump which they almost shoved in your face, they asked; *Baksi ibvendi*, alms sir!

The Islamic faith requires that you give alms to the needy. Beggars make use of it and believe me as a festering stump, covered with flies is held to your face, then you do not know how fast you unearth a few piastres out of your pocket. 'Always ensure that you have small change on you,' was an advice of my father, who had spent most years of his life in the tropics. We struggled through the crowd and came to the office my father's company. I stood waiting outside and waved automatically a fly from my lip. A moment later he came out and we walked back through the Souk to our car. 'It's warm,' my father said. 'The weather is going to turn'. 'Are you eating enough salt,' asked my father? 'Think about it, huh? Your body loses a lot of salt when you sweat'. My father was at that time still a nice father, but then we could not know what would be waiting for us on the horizon. He was careful in his ways and gave good advice. I could not have imagined at that time, that we would be at utterly bad terms within five years from then.'You know what', he suggested,' when we have f nished at the post office we will take something to drink, because in this weather you lose a lot of moisture.' That seemed like a good plan and I looked proudly at my father, who always took care of everything and was great.

In Libya his length was very much noticed, he was about 6 foot six, and that was for his generation impressive. He was strong, you simply knew that, he just radiated it out and he had a very dominant personality. When he stepped into a room, he just radiated out power. He was present. The drink did not take place, because sometimes things go differently than you expect.

We got in the car and my father had released the handbrake. At that time it was a kind of hook, that you had to reinsert. He reached into his shirt pocket for cigarettes and I saw a group of chattering young Arabs approaching. From a rich class, you could see that from their robes. The front one was too busy talking and laughing and turned half around to say something to a friend. His foot got caught in the hem of his long cloak and he stumbled, stepped forward and hit with the side of his head the rain gutter of our car.

He collapsed next to the car all together. A great commotion broke loose. Some men dragged my father out of the car and I think he would have been lynched if a police car had not stopped at that time, to see what was going on. Someone started shouting that the Americanos had run into the boy. My father got a corrective slap with the bat when he wanted to say something, and was taken away handcuffed. It all happened quickly, I could not even get out. I took the key from the ignition lock and felt very composed. I locked the car and began to walk home, the few kilometers back.

Cell phones did not exist and there was nothing to do but walk. The first thing my mother cried when she saw me was,'where's Dad? 'I told her as good and as bad as I could, what I thought had happened. My mother called the consulate and the Oasis Oil Company. My father's company always had a small army of lawyers ready to smother problems in the bud Everyone assured my mother that she should not need to worry that they would solve everything. It was after two days that Muhammad, the garden boy came to report that my father had been transferred to Puerto Bonito. Puerto Bonito was the prison for severe cases. It was a 19th century brick outlet, a legacy of the Italian regime, when Libya had been a colony to Italy.

The employee of the consulate was not admitted. The lawyer of the Oasis Company, neither. Meanwhile, my father was already four days in custody. Muhammad asked after the fifth day if we had brought my father anything to eat. Family members bring food and drink to the prisoners. Not that you see them, you leave it behind with the head guard in his lodge and then he brings it, you hope, to the relevant prisoner. Mohammed knew an awful lot about the ins and outs of being in prison .. Always leave cigarettes behind, for the guards, he advised, that tunes them favorable. Oh, and about half pack too much, then maybe there will be some that reach your husband.

My poor, dear mother almost succumbed, when she heard that. Put enough chocolate in, knew our Mohammed, the other prisoners will like that. You will make friends that way. Every day Muhammad was off with the dandelion taxi to the prison. Puerto Bonito is no place for children, he said, and you should definitely not go, as a woman, because the guards are not much used to women, Women should not be on the streets anyway and certainly not come in such places. He meant that they were sadistic, Machian, bastards.

After two weeks, a lawyer was admitted and he told my mother that my father had lost a lot of weight but to circumstances appeared to be in good condition. However, he would like to have a change, because he still had the same clothes on as the day of his arrest. Discussion and talks went on but to no avail. The company wanted to pay a deposit, but they did not want to accept that. After three months, my father was still in Puerto Bonito. My mother got a note from one of the guards, given to Mohammed, along with the empty food basket, in which my father asked for some small articles. A piece of soap and flea powder, I tend to remember and some other stuff. In the fourth month, the miracle happened. The young Arab who had walked against the gutter of the car, blinked and came out of his coma. He was immediately questioned and he stated that he had tripped and had fallen against a parked car with his head Then you would expect that everything was resolved. In a normal country with a normal law system yes, in Libya, no. The judiciary had a problem with my father, an innocent man had for months, been imprisoned without trial. In America, he could've sued to kingdom come.

Ah, there are always solutions to problems, God willing. One day my father had to appear in court and fortunately a lawyer from the firm was allowed to be present, and he had to pay a sum of 250 pounds. I'm talking about 1963, that was then; 2500 guilders, a small fortune. My father wanted to protest, but the lawyer of Oasis constricted his mouth. He seems to have said.'if you want to ever see the light of day again, keep your mouth shut'. The lawyer asked if it was a fine. But the judge responded that the costs had been for the hospitality that my father had enjoyed in Puerto Bonito. They had watched over him to prevent the young Arab to be avenged.

The lawyer thanked the court and wrote a check from the company and my father was a free man again. In a country like Libya a white or a non-Muslim, has no rights. Oasis Oil Company, paid the family a week Malta and the next day we were in a plane of *Bea* on the way to the airport in La Valetta. My father has never let loose one word about his stay in Puerto Bonito, which suggests that it must have been a dismal experience.

The waterfall of Tarhuna

The calendar that my father had received as a company gift, showed per month a beautiful photograph of some Libyan attraction. The American company that my father worked for, did everything to present the host country, Libya, as positive as possible .. The first photo on the cover, was a little less attractive, it showed an old man next to the Libyan flag with an Arabic text next to it. The Arabic text was translated into English, below the photograph. *King Idris, defender of The Faith, King Idris protector of the faith*. 'With syrup you'll catch more flies than with vinegar,' the public relations man of the company must have thought.

The 78-year-old defender of the faith, looked worn down, in a way that did not particularly give you a happy, positive feeling and then they had probably selected the best picture of him. There was no denying he was lurking down at you from the calendar. That gave his appearance something sinister, you do not want a lurking pope on your calendar, either now do you? The company had meant well but the cover photo, did not inspire confidence, in the protector of the faith.

Oh, my mother said, you should see this as she was paging through the calendar, and pointed at a photo of a waterfall of unprecedented size. An accompanying text stated that this was the pride of the environment; the waterfall of TARHUNA. That looks beautiful, my father agreed. In a country where the heat prevails and where flies are part of any area where you go and where there is always dust swirling in the air, a cool stream, let alone a waterfall, is a God's gift. A waterfall in all it's splendour, as shown on the calendar of the Oasis Oil Company, certainly was. It invited in its pristine freshness, to sit down next to it and just, feel at the foot of the fall, the spray of splashing water that would soak you wet. It almost conjured up lyrical images. Humans and water are connected, water gives life. My brother and I were 'tough' and would not be so quick with Ooohs and Aaahs, but to be honest, it looked attractive. Couldn't we go there some time, asked my mother, who never came out of the house because you don't, Western women in Libya do not leave the house ever. Libyans are not used to women alone on the street.

Her outings consisted of monthly gambling with my father in the Waddan, the casino in Tripoli, or Wheelus Airbase where we attended every Sunday a Lutheran church service in the offi cer's mess. Wheelus airbase was a bit a displaced civilization behind barbed wire. Americans and Europeans were given a pass on request, to attend services. It was not so much the church service which was pleasant, a church service is a church service. And you could actually go to a church service, which was impossible outside the base. In a country where every two hours throughout the day, an Imam yells from the minarets *that Allah is great and there is no God other than Allah,* you simply leave it out of your mind to found a church. That equates to signing your death warrant.

It was a welcome distraction. You were just back amongst the us feeling. you could talk freely, women could just walk around in this bit of transplanted and moved America. An oasis of peace in a country where the hatred against whites ricocheted off your head, where ever you walked. You felt not hated for that little while. You were again *amongst us*, in your own tribe. The service ways consisted of two hyms and a reading by Captain Mackletan, the fighter pilot, who had assumed the role of pastor. The captain did not like to elborate and most services did not last longer than 20 minutes. Then invariably followed by coffee and donuts. We were the outpost of Western civilization, but curiously enough behind barbed wire. Twice a month Captain Mackletan organized a barbeque, because he loved them himself and on the other remaining Sundays, there was a buffet made by the church ladies. My mother looked always very much forward to that and baked the preceding week, that it was a delight. Everyone prepared a dish and took it and placed it on a long table and then everyone ate together. That is the way churches ought to be! That is what Jesus must have meant, I thought years later. No endless praying and preaching. No, a meeting where you decide to say that you still believe in all the same values and then you'd have a nice time together.

The church was the reason that was used to eradicate the outside Arabic world, and strengthen your mind and when you drove back from Wheelus Airbase, passing the checkpoints, you were recharged for a week in order to cope with the hate again.

'I will try to find out at the office, where exactly this TARHUNA is', replied my father. But if we go, then we do so on a Saturday and not on a Sunday because I do not want to miss the service. He was probably referring to the barbeque or buffet, where the men were then assembled with a beer in hand, passing jokes or just stood around relaxed together sharing stories. Today it is hard to imagine, but outside the Airbase you could not drink a single beer. *Allahhhh. Allahhhh* is great, it sounded amplified from the minarets of the city, which you barely noticed because it had become part of the background noise *ie Allahh. Alahhh h* and Mohammed is his prophet. Mohammed was our gardener !!

One evening my father said that he knew where to find TARHUNA and that the distance was not too bad. It was about 80 kilometers west of Tripoli. In a normal country 80 kilometers is chicken little, but just outside Tripoli the asphalt roads stop. This has its advantages and disadvantages. Where there is asphalt you need to watch for the huge holes in the road. The asphalt roads are not well maintained and trucks drive the roads to pieces. But you do not throw up dust clouds. Sometimes you're better off without asphalt. Asphalt roads in Africa have the nasty side effect that they attract snakes. Often cobra's lay their heads are on the road and their bodies hidden in the sand, drowsy to warm up. We left early and had a few flasks of water along, because you never knew what could happen.

Just outside Tripoli the roads simply stopped. There was a "piste" through the desert. A hard-ridden dirt road, levelled out occasionally by a bulldozer and then sprayed with used oil. The latter had evidently already happened some time ago, because wherever you went you were chased by clouds of dust. You saw the scarce oncoming traffic coming from afar. Then in passing each party whipped up a mini sandstorm. There was occasionally at an intersection, a sign in Arabic. My mother was a bit worried and asked, shall we go back, if we are surprised by a sand storm, we are lost.' My father played the role he had always ascribed to himself, the role of adventurer. 'We', he said emphatically, can not get lost'. 'Oh', my mother replied, 'and what makes you think so'?'Because we follow the railroad line', and he pointed to my mother's side and indeed the attentive observer could now see an increase in the sand, of what had once been an embankment.

'This is the old railway line, he clarified that connects Tripoli with TARHUNA. It was built during the Italian period, when Libya was an Italian colony.' We listened intently. My father was a walking source of knowledge. 'In 1943,' my father said,' the British defeated General Rommel's units and Italy lost, as an ally of Germany, her colony. The battles in the desert have been very violent. They crossed the desert seven times back and forth, conquering and then losing ground again.

In the distance we saw a silhouette stabbing out of the sand and my father stopped the car. We were able to stretch their legs and walked to the piece of steel that rose up out of the sand. It was an old steam locomotive. My father immediately began a lecture on maintenance and how unfortunate it was that a country that gets handed over a railway from a former ruler, in turn lets it go to waste. Libyans are simply not technical. They live in another era, and I could see that my dad was right there.

We had driven quite a bit when we saw ruins in the distance. I've heard about this,' my father said, 'from the boys at the office, those are ancient Roman ruins. That means that we are going right fine'. The drought and the lack of acidy rain had made sure that the Roman ruins in the interior of Africa were in a far better condition than many a retreat in the Roman Forum. We saw in the distance a man standing on a hilltop. If the road is straight and long, you notice minimal differences instantaneously. He waved to a far distance and blew a horn. The image of Indians on a hilltop in the Wild West forced itself on me. Would he have blown a horn at that time if we had not come along, I wondered?

The road made a few twists and we saw a village looming. People came from the cabin-style homes and put themselves on either side of the road. You felt doom approaching, but there was only one way. My father slowed down and the dust cloud that we left behind us declined dramatically. The stones rained down and made a star in the windshield, while we went charging past. My father raced on with tight lips behind the wheel.'That was a Berber village,' my father said, unnecessary for us he continued, 'careful with Berbers, you can not trust them'. As if anyone would want to trust a stone-throwing Berber. ' The problem is

that we have to take this road back again,' continued my father.

'Well fi rst things first TARHUNA here we come.' It was not long before we arrived at the first sign of civilization. Small children, who looked very unkempt, waved friendly to us. My father stopped at a tavern with a signboard that unmistakably recommended Coke, in Arabic. You recognize the logo anywhere. It was the first vegetation, an oasis-like area. '*Gamsa cola vadlek, ivendi*,' my father asked in carefull measured out words, of the owner. Five cola please, sir.' Are you American,' asked the man smiling? 'No,' my father said, but we do speak English. 'What brings you here,' the man asked? My mother opened her Mary Popin's bag and pulled out the calendar and she gave it to my father. My father pointed at the picture and asked if it was still far.' Hmm,' the man said, and he looked again and got someone to have a look, who looked and shook his head. Now a third man came standing and pointing and a whole conversation took place until the barman's face lit up. My father wanted to be helpful,' it lies in TARHUNA,' he explained.

'This is TARHUNA,' said the boss of the coffee bar. 'I think we know where this is' the man said, 'but you will never find it by yourself.' ' Please note that my son is a guide'. He shouted something with many guttural sounds and which sounded unintelligible to us, at least I understood nothing. A young boy of around 10 years old now came walking in. *'I guide, I guide,'* he cried friendly and he patted his chest.'Right', said my father. 'What does your guide cost?" He drives with you and shows you what you want to see and you bring him back here, said the owner of the bar.' 'Yes,' said my father, now a bit more insistent, 'what do his services cost?' For you, only two pounds,' the man replied, smiling from ear to ear with a bow. '*You spit on my house,*' my father said, with a lot of clamor. '*You insult my village and you crush my barn.*' 'I only want one guide, not your whole family. I will pay 50 piastres, and that's a favor.'It's my favorite son', replied the owner, and he raised his hands to heaven, 'but you are not American,' 'I will let him go for a pound and a half." *You're kicking my donkey',* my father said, 75 piastres, 'and no more insults'!' Forward 1 pound then', was the reply from the owner' and we will not talk about it anymore.' My father paid one pound.

We left with the minature guide after finishing our cokes. After five minutes, he made it clear that we had to stop, and he pointed to a spot under a tree. My father parked the car in the shade of it and we followed our young guide. The path led down to the bank of a small stream. The boy looked very proud and pointed to the stream.' Oh, Oh,', said my mother, and took out of the depths of her bag the calendar and she pointed at the picture of the waterfall. He beckoned us and made his way along what thickets of the oasis and pointed ahead. There was the same rock formation as of the calendar and down them trickled a waterfall 50 inches wide. 'Exactly,' said my father,' it was to be expected, taken by a Berber photographer, can´t miss.'

'Aah,' said my mother, 'it's really very beautiful'. 'It is smaller than in the picture, though, but maybe that was taken in the rainy season.' She took off her shoes and stood in the stream. And I? I loved her so much. So terribly much, that it included everything around us, a love so pure, the stream, the boy, the few green bushes, opened my heart and it f ew around her. 'This,' said my father, 'is the country where nothing is what it seems.

'Late, very much later we came home and we all looked forward to the barbeque, the next day after church and it was one of the few f ne experience in that dry barren land. Probably it is such a nice memory because it is one of the last times that I saw my mother in good health, before the cowardly hand of a terrible disease began to proliferate her out of our lives. We would then trudge for years, lost through life.

Sweet teachers

The house where we lived was paid for by the oil company. It was on the outskirts of Tripoli. It was a large house with a garden on three sides. The garden was surrounded by a larger-than- life wall and in the garden two tall palm trees waved in a warm breeze and a dried citrus tree, had shrivelled away in a corner. It was in a U-shaped complex of similar houses. Little pitchers have big ears and I remember that the man from the oil company who went along to show houses named a price. My head has always been into numbers.

The rent of the house was £ 400 per month. That meant nothing to me then. Now, so many years later it has become quite meaningful. That house cost at the beginning of the 60's, when the pound was still ten guilders, 4000 guilders per month. The equivalent of ten one month salaries in Holland at the time. The house had a hall adjoining reception area, a lounge in addition to the kitchen, bathroom and three bedrooms. The whole was perhaps 10 by 10 meters so that the total surface area was 100 square meters. Everything was expensive in Tripoli for the "rich" foreigners. Believe you me, the house did not justify the rent.It made no difference to the company, they wanted anyway that the oil boys, the real technicians, were satisfied. That if they were flown into the wilderness to work there for a week on and then have week off, they were not concerned about their families. During the week, that my father was off the desert shift, he would go to the main building in Tripoli where he shared a small office with two other Oil engineers. There was a lot of demand in the world for people who were really in the know about the nitty gritty of the oil business and Libya was not a pleasant place to live.

After a few days my father said to me,' tomorrow, I'll walk you to the Shell school, which is only two blocks away and then you can start school life again.' I never disliked school and the elementary school that I had left in the Netherlands gave me pleasant memories. At that time the classes were large and there were only six classes of elementary school because the kindergarten period was not integrated with the primary school with two girls and another boy, I met two times a week a bit earlier before school started and the headmaster who held a degree in French and English, then gave us an extra hour of tuition. On a Friday afternoon, the same boy and two girls and I remained behind a bit longer and we got the same headmaster, who then became a calculation wonder, and gave us the principles of algebra, he steamed us ready for high school, the *real* high school, as he would say. He led us into the world of prime numbers and taught us square roots. Roots that worked out.

To this end, we paid two quarters a lesson, two coins that you put at the corner of your table. During the explanations he walked past and put the money in his pocket. It was a protestant Christian school and he had hand picked us. In his words, which were not very educational, he had shifted the wheat from the chaff. I suppose we were the wheat.

At a time when the 'A' level tests did not yet exist, and masters and teachers were plagued by 40 pupils in a class and children still could fail classes, we were his hour of rest in the week. We were those children, that were really interested and understood what he said. Here he could share his knowledge and what a luxury, to only four children, the difference was great with the other pupils and the word of the headmaster was sacred, and his advice was always followed. He would refer children to a technical school and if they were boys, to a vocational school, girls were sent to a domestic school to learn how to cook and how to iron,or some like us were to be sent to what he's so nicely called, *the real* high school. We were meant to enter through the portals of the real high school. His word was never questioned.Now the focus is much more on little children with learning difficulties, in order to uplift them with extra tasks. When the teacher of class 5 drew attention to his favorites and the headmaster in the sixth grade embroidered on and focused on those few, who in his eyes could eventually become his equals, your lot was cast.

Society was very different 50 years ago. I was curious about what the Shell school would be like, especially curious about the the schoolmates that I'd meet.. Maybe a few lived in my neighbourhood, because I missed my friends that I had left behind suddenly. Such is the life of oil men, They are "suitcase" people. Suitcase packed? We'll see where the next contract takes us.

The experts always repeat in another place the same trick against an exaggerated wage. They'd move somewhere, they'd build within four years a heavy technical project, They'd run a one year trial period to debug the whole lot and then the transfer would follow and … they'd go somewhere … For the children, that were taken out of their environment where they had just settled in, it was different, they were taken away to a new country to start all over again.

It was the beginning of a hot day and my father and I walked on to the street. I felt tense and uncertain but cherished the expectation of the adventure. 'Pay attention,' my father said, 'you have to walk back home yourself and if you get lost, there is no one who understands you. and then we will never see you again.' After a few turns and winding streets we arrived at Calle Benghazi, crossed over and after another few confusing streets we faced a fenced in villa. I had really observed well how we had walked, as I did not want to be lost forever in an Arabic country.

It looked repulsively unfriendly. A heavy fence with gate that was locked with a bell next to it. A wall that enclosed everything with on top spikes on a railing. It looked like a prison camp when you walked in. A garden boy opened the gate and we walked to the wide front door. I remember that I thought; in the name of William Orange, open up that gate. When my father banged on the door. A friendly-looking lady appeared, she smiled at my father with a heavenly smile. My father always had that effect on women. He always radiated: *intelligent prehistoric man*. Women always would swoon, They would hear the distant aah aah oe HHA oooe a primal roar of Tarzan and saw a civilized figure who mockingly dealt with the world.

The world was his oyster'I had been expecting you', said the lady who probably was unmarried and saw a potential prey in front of her. 'Oh, not too long I should hope', smiled my father , while he took her outstretched hand and kissed it lightly. The teacher, because that is what she turned out to be, blushed deep into her neck. Romeo that he was, nothing had happened, but I felt the betrayal to my mother. I despised him at such moments. Always that f irting and fooling around and meanwhile quite the civilized gentleman. The man of the world. Later I would learn that there is an English name for his appearance: a lady's man.

There is a type of woman that can smell power and money and if that possibility is attractively packaged in a person then they act like a magnet. All the more, if such a man is unattainable, because of an earlier commitment. That makes such men irresistibly attractive. Later in a study Historical literature I would understand it better, it had a name,the motivations of *Courtly Love. Unattainable love.* 'Shall we come in,' continued my father, and without waiting for an answer, he pushed me with his hand my neck in front of him. 'This is my son, Daniel,' said my father solemnly. 'Would you like some tea said the teacher, I'm just about to have some myself'. 'Unfortunately', my father said, 'I must decline', I have to settle urgent matters at the office.' He bowed slightly, as if he took leave of the queen and said 'mylady,' with a nod of his head. The teacher looked at him for a moment and closed the door. 'Your father is a true gentleman,' she found it necessary to say, 'would you like some tea, young Daniel?' she meant to say,' I thought, 'your dad was really gorgeous,' but I said, 'No thank you madam, I would not want to trouble you.' 'Oh', she said, 'you are just like your father,' and time has put her right since, I have become my father but without the ugly traits.

There were two dining tables in a room and there were a total of 14 children around. That was the whole school! My old protestant reformed headmaster would have drooled for joy. Unfortunately, that working educator had to do with the sparse quarters at the corners of the tables of the elect. I was introduced and the children looked up briefly. Everyone had a cup of tea with a biscuit beside him. Not to be imagined.' Vanity of vanities,' my headmaster, God rest his soul, would have said.

This was the only class with all levels in a room. Table 1 was for the youngsters say to nine years and table two, from my father's teacher let's say, had the older children, that is where I was placed.. I was given a sheet with some fractions, Unbelievably easy, a few percentage sums and the all famous: Peet leaves at a rate 8 kilometers per hour to travel a range of 30 kilometers, his friend John departs 12 minutes later with a speed of 10 kilometers per hour, where and when do they .. It took me a very short time indeed to finish my sheet, and I handed it in. Here you have a language exercise said my father's teacher. Meanwhile, I'll check you work.

A moment later my sheet was returned, a big curl was put over the leaf, such a weird old sign from past days meaning, good, or well done!. Nothing wrong, what did you expect, my parents had not paid the quarters for nothing to the headmaster! I had finished my language exercise, and my father's teacher, started checking it. 'That is very good,' she said, satisfied. 'Here is a book, and go and sit outside to read.' There I was in the sun with a booklet, Could you believe it, a booklet which we had read at my old school in the third grade; Jacob and Gert, it could not be more square. There I was drowsily bored. It was clear, here, I was not going learn much here.

The door opened and a boy came out, 'I am Cor,' he said, and held out his hand. I shook his hand and asked, 'are you allowed to read as well?' 'I am always allowed to read,' he replied. 'I take books with me from my own home.' 'Oh,' I said, I thought that was a good idea. 'Can I see it,' I asked? It was a book with a picture of the jungle on it, and an adventurer with a machete chopping up a monstrous snake. *Bob Morane*, it said, *and the secret temple*. That sounded really good to me. 'I've read it twice already,' said Cor, 'do you want to borrow it'? 'Please, thank you,' I said.'It does not matter what you do here,' he told me, you're always promoted to the next form. I've been here three years now'. 'Next year my parents go to Oman, then I'll go to the same sort of school like the one here, but only in Oman". Oh,' I said.' We are parked, you know,' he said. 'Parents send us to school and we are taken care of.' 'No,' I replied,' my dad really wants me to learn something'. 'Well,' smiled Cor,'that's what you think, he has his own life, he has formally taken care of you.' Only much later, when Cor was long gone and out of sight, I realized he was right.

It was afternoon and the school went out. The teacher came out and unlocked the gate. She gave me a note and said, would you give this to your father, if he has any questions he can call me. A car with a chauffeur came and picked Cor pick up. We waved when he drove away. I decided when I'd get home I would immediately enlighten myself with Bob Morane and his secret temple.

I unfolded the note. The text was innocent but loaded. You can always call me .. followed by a number .. I threw the note away, I knew again what time of day it was. Then I walked in home. 'So' asked my father, who wanted to show interest when I got home, 'how did you get on?' 'Well,' I answered, 'I did some sums and spelling and then I was allowed to play outside.' 'Long', asked my father? 'A few hours I replied.'The next day I gave the book back to Cor. I had to do some sums and do a sheet of language exercises and a little later I was allowed to play outside again. After three days, my father became suspicious. Why do you always get to play outside, he asked, 'my schooltime was very different." I do not know,' I replied. 'I've been getting everything right, and then I'm done.' Right', said my father. I knew from experience that my father had then reached a verdict. 'Tomorrow I'll come with you,' he said.

We walked through the door and the swooning teacher looked at my dad with love in her eyes. 'My son says he can play outside during class time,' my father said. 'That's right,' said the teacher, 'he is very good, he knows everything.' 'Right,' said my father, and with a small bow of his head we disappeared from her life.

'Tomorrow I have to check on some projects in the desert', my father said, 'Next week we'll go to a real school.' These words reminded me of my old headmaster.' I am going to enroll you in the O.C.S'. said my father, 'The American Oil Company School'. 'You do not speak English,' he said', but you'll pick it up.' I nodded meekly, Resistance had no use. I sat down in the garden and thought, I won't even see Cor again. I envied the chicken that walked around freely in our garden, if I were only that chicken I thought...

The yellow bus and the OCS

'Tomorrow you must be ready well in time,' my mother said,'your father has enrolled you in the Oil Company School.' 'How do I get there, I asked with some concern?' 'You'll go by bus, my mother said firmly. The school is just outside Giorgimpopoli.' 'Bloody hell,'I thought, 'have they all gone mad? I do not speak the language and I'm supposed to go a place I do not know, and I've never heard of, to find it located just outside of that other place by bus. 'Is there anyone coming along,' I asked timidly? 'No, your father will remain some days longer in the desert and I have no driver's license,' my mother said. I could say good morning in English and ask for the time of day and count from one to ten, and that was about it.

'You do not look very happy,' my mother said,' go and take a seat.' 'The company sends a bus past, a big yellow bus.' You need to wait outside the fence and when the bus arrives, you raise your hand and you get in. That bus will take you to school and then you follow the rest of the kids. Somewhere there, you'll see an office and you hand them a letter which I'm writing now. You will be expected, and they'll show you the way to class. I have always loved to have control over events, and I understood that I was handed over to fate. In our family, opinions were not asked for, I realized that I had no choice.

'School starts early and ends at two o'clock', my mother continued. 'They have to, because of the heat.' 'I didn't know what you might need but I had your brother buy you a lunchbox, I've put something to drink and some food in it, because at school you cannot buy anything.' 'There seems to be a buzzer when school is out and then you quickly go, to where you have stepped off the bus and if things go well, that same bus brings you back home.' Now I really began to worry.

That night I slept poorly, I worried about people that I would not understand and busses that had to be there but had already left. The morning light came into my room and I got up reluctantly. My mother was already sitting at the dinner table with her dressing gown on. She looked approvingly at me and mother's inherent in every country in the world, she fiddled a bit with my shirt, brushed my hair straight and gave me a kiss. 'Have a good day,' she said as she pushed me to the door.. I held a lunch box with a handle in my hands and a moment later I was standing outside.

It was still early and I found it ever so fresh in my shorts. There were no flies that early, they would come out later when the sun would start to warm our street up. It was quiet on the streets, it was normally a quiet street, but there was no life at all to be seen at this time of day. The silence, however, wore away by a sound and I heard the bus arrive, it appeared around the corner. It was a big yellow bus, with a sign 'school bus' on it. I raised my hand and it stopped right beside me. The door hissed open and a fat matronne, beckoned me pouring a torrent of words over me. Behind me the doors shut again and the bus immediately set in motion..

I was nearly thrown over by the bus racing away. The matronne pushed me to a place and said something I did not understand. I looked around me and I immediately noticed the first difference between me and the other children. The boys all had long pants on. A boy nudged his neighbor and pointed to me, how could it be, he pointed at my lunchbox, yes, I was the only one with a Donald Duck lunchbox.

The rest of the children had lunch boxes in a solid color with a large rubber band around it. My Donald Duck creation f ipped open, and then in the upper part I had a thermos and sandwiches and a fruit down below. My caring mother also had put a napkin in it. I had a problem, I knew it, I would have that lunchbox until eternity, my parents, would not see the need to buy me another one, boy I had a problem. Meanwhile the fat lady shouted her head off to the children in a language I did not understand. I assumed that she was Italian, because it just did not sound English.

When I spoke broken English six months later, I knew she was Italian and it was her job to keep children quiet so that the driver was not distracted. She screamed and yelled at no end. Where the bus stopped she pulled the children inside. I felt severely unhappy and feigned a huge interest in the outside world. I looked all the way out of the window. The bus rumbled by and stormed through small villages. Eventually, the driver slowed down and he drove on to a large sandy area and parked the bus near a huge wall. There were four other yellow buses. A year later, I understood that they were real American school buses that had been transferred by the Oasis Oil company to Libya. The oil companies were not a miserable lot.

The complex was quite a ways inside the gate and the children came from all directions pouring in. It was a huge complex. Everything was ground level, of course there was land enough, so why build a school with levels? Everyone was on his way to his classroom. It was a cluster of long barrack-like buildings. The roofs were not flat but slightly sloping. The whole complex was built on an elevated platform half a meter above ground level. Later I understood the logic behind it, it complicated scorpions and other vermin access to school.

The image that comes to mind is a comb with four teeth. The handle of the comb length. Between those legs were strips of dried, about 10 yards wide. The wall which ran parallel to the strip of dry soil was a glass wall. That was also the wall where the roof was the highest. The handle portion which was at odds with the length barracks, housed the off ce. In front of the office was a tall flagpole flying the American flag. That was where I needed to go. I walked over to it, pushing myself through the mass of deodorant smells and entered the office which was divided into two parts by a counter that ran over the entire length. Several ladies were typing. It was the vicious hard ticking sound you hear nowhere nowadays.

Another lady took some notes in from students. This was a piece of America that had been moved behind the fences of Libya. It was my turn and suddenly I realized how bad it had to be, to be mute. I introduced myself: I am Daniel, good morning and I held the letter from my mother out, it was taken by a kind lady with a big smile. I understood:' a very good morning to you too, Daniel ..' but the rest went over my head.

The letter was brought to a seperate office and a moment later a man came out who said something to me, and beckoned me. My non-verbal remark capacity running at full speed to compensate for what I did not understand in language. My hand was shaken and I was spoken to in a deep American voice. I did not understand any of it. I did notice that the lips of the speaker barely moved.

Now, I know that Texans have that, they do not articulate much and that is why they speak with a "drawl", which is elongated and sounds lazy. Thus, 'why boy', becomes pronounced by Texans *'waah Bohh?* Oh well you get used to everything in life. Now, much later, I could have walked in Texas, and no one would have recognized me as non Texan. Without liprounding, vowels get a stretched sound. I took over the Texan drawl, because you want to fit in as quickly as possible now, don't you? *'Cause you wanna fit in, ya hear?*

He got up and grabbed me by my shoulder and walked me back to the counter. He said something with the word *son* in it, and gave me into the hands of an employee who beckoned me and indicated that I should follow her. She brought me to a closed door and knocked on it and came inside with me. The children all looked up to see who the new kid was. The master sat on a platform and stopped talking and walked to the door. He held out his hand and I shook it and said, I am Daniel. He looked at me and repeated what I had said and added something to it. I am Daniel, **sir .. sir**, and he put a lot of emphasis on **sir..** he took me by my shoulder in a fatherly way, and set me down in front of him.

It was not a fun day. The teacher's name was Mr. Harper and if anyone ever helped me in a school then it was this man who was strict and was but as didactic person had a heart of gold. God rest his soul. Somebody raised his finger a bit later to ask something;' Mister Harper, sir can I ... 'and I understood that the man's name, was Harper. The boy next to me was addressed by Mr. Harper and after some gestures I understood that he had been put in charge over me. They all had books and I had nothing.

The boy next to me seemed to be called Keith and I understand now that he was the laughing stock of the class because he did not come from Texas. So we formed a nice couple. The buzzer went three times and everyone got up, the boy next to me poked me in the side and I got up as well. They all stood straight up and looked blurry far ahead of them. They folded their right fist and laid it on their hearts. Mr. Harper was standing in front of the class and also had his hand on his heart and looked just as blurry eyed.

Mr.Harper began to recite something and everyone supported him. I had no idea what it all was about. It was as if you were in a church service where a creed was repeated in an incomprehensible language. When in Rome do like the Romans, I moved my lips, and I had my hand on my heart. I felt like a moron and I could have screamed with rage. I had been silenced.

When the bell went at the end of the lesson, I walked along with Keith. I was the only one who walked with my lunchbox, what had the rest done with their lunchbox? We had to go to another leg of the comb. A group of boys in my class came standing around me and asked me something while we were waiting at the still closed door. I laughed a bit sheepishly, the speaker then kicked my lunchbox out of my hands.

The others began to laugh. Keith looked the other way. I got a push and when I wanted to get at my attacker, another boy kicked me from behind. A blond girl said something, I think she had stood up for me, now I was really being kicked. Against my shins, from behind in my back. I was hit on the head.. Texan boys determine your place and station, they are from the lone star state, and with many they are 'really tough.' It was the punishment for someone for not being from Texas. *Ride Em Cowboy yi haah* !! Just my luck. I had all the school bullies in my class. Suddenly, just as quickly as it had started it stopped.

A lovely appearance came walking with a key in her hand. Keith said something and pushed me forward. I said as I reached my hand out, 'Good Morning, I am Daniel, sir'. Behind the bullies burst out in hard laughter. I am Miss Johnson, said the lady, with a big smile, she would be my great love among the teachers that terrible first year. 'I am your French teacher.' It turned out to be a French lesson. Great! Thanks to the efforts of my quarters loving headmaster of before, I knew how to conjugate the verbs avoir and être. Miss Johnson was very nice.

She spoke her English differently. Later in life I would recognize her accent as the accent of someone from Michican. We all had to take turns reading and I watched and she beamed when It had been my turn to read. The rest of my classmates sounded terribly American and I really sounded almost French. We had to learn the lessons by heart. All lessons treated certain themes. I still know them.

Jéntre dans la salle de classe, you regarde autour de mois, je vois les élèves et le professeur, je dis bonjour a professeur et je prends ma place ..I understood after a few seconds what I had done wrong when I had presented myself earlier. Students raised their hand and began, 'Miss Johnson, Ma'm..' I wrote it down. Ma'm is madam or teacher.

Sir is master. The boy next to me said it differently, and asked, 'Miss Johnson, madam ..' So an arrow on my notepad on my notepad pointing to ma'm and madam = teacher. When the final bell rang I was spent, I was dead tired. Keith unfortunately did not take my bus. I recognized the bus from afar by the matronne that sat next to it with a list in her hand, which she checked off as a child got on. I was empty, I had really had a bad day. I had been laughed at, I had been pushed and kicked and beaten and I had almost gone deaf mute. I felt a rage inside me over the undeserved injustice that was done to me. I could not even ask if I could go to the toilet. When the bus stopped my mother was standing in the garden watering some plants.' And,' she asked,' did you enjoy your first day of school on the OCS?' 'Oh Yeah, very nice,' I said, because I did not want her to know what a wretch I had become. 'Really,' she asked? She could always read me like a book, 'No,' I said, 'it was awful.'

'I'll make you some tea,'she said' and then tell me about it' and she walked with me to the kitchen .. I left the kicking and taunting out of my story.' I'm proud of you,' she said,' it cannot have been very nice.' 'You have no idea,' I said. 'Well..,' my mother replied, ' actually I have and your father as well.' I must have looked surprised.

Your father was of Dutch parents, born in Java and he did not have a nice schooltime, he had to learn Malay. When he had finished school he was sent alone to the Netherlands to study and he had to live in rooms. At that time I met your father, He was not Indo nor half cast and not Dutch. He was a stray in a lost land. 'I had the same,' she said. I probably looked even more surprised. 'I was born in Franeker', she continued, 'and my father, your grandfather, found work in Haarlem because at that time there was no work for him in Friesland. I just spoke Frisian and golly jee , believe me, it has been very difficult in the West, where only Dutch was spoken.' Suddenly I looked at my parents with different eyes. 'You know what is nice', my mother asked?' Your dad can still speak Malay' and I can still speak Frisian. We can move in other worlds. For a time it is not nice, after a while you won't know better. She was right, I now know: *mooi zoid*, let's say, in Frisian looking back now after so many years.

The pledge:

The bus came five days a week and I learned a lot. On Monday morning you were to wait on arrival at the flagpole. The American flag was then hoisted and you recited***: I am proud to be an American, protector of the poor, defender of the free*** .. Everyone knew it by heart and spoke the words without feelings of shame. After a few months, the words had meaning to me and I began to identify with them. Then you'd put the right hand, fist clenched, on your heart and repeated the pledge to the American flag. ***I pledge allegiance to the flag of the United States of America, and to the republic for All which it stands, one nation under God, indivisible, with liberty and justice for all.***

On other days you waited until the buzzer went three times and then you got up in your room with your classmates and repeated the same ritual. It created a feeling of unity. Mr. Harper had arranged my books. He was my homeroom teacher, say my tutor and so I gradually became more familiar with the rites and customs of the OCS. I had been assigned a locker with a combination of numbers and my gym clothes went in there together with my Donald Duck lunchbox.

My Texan tormentors were for a time very annoying and I could be pestered almost unlimited, there was no end to the bullying and hitting and kicking. Because ... *Danny cannot tell the teacher* ... they were a bunch of sick dogs and I hated them. Everyone got a number on the back of his gymshirt and on the belly. My number was 41 That number corresponded with your name, on a clipboard in the hands of our physical education teacher. Our teacher was Mr. Kelly, he was convinced that you had to make men out of boys, and he was under the impression that we wanted to be US marines. We did a lot of abdominal exercises, sit-ups, push-ups a lot of times, push-ups and running, always running.

He did not run himself, he was on a small elevated platform with binoculars and a megaphone. If you ran in that heat, it was bad enough. Your body temperature is 36 degrees. If you are going to run in 45 degrees then you will not lose the surplus warmth and your body temperature flies up. You get over heated, with red cheeks and a dry throat you tried to finish, the laps around the sandy fi eld. If you fell behind, he saw because of your number who you were and roared through the megaphone 'his encouragement'. He had been coach of a rugby team in the states and knew no mercy. We ran in the blood heat with a mister Kelly who 'cheered' us on, over the field his voice would roar. Using foul language. The megaphone went on and while you'd have in the back of your mouth a blood taste and your throat was desert dry he would scream at you. ' Number 5, Pitman, *Get you ass in gear .. put your ass in gear.* The man was a savage brute. If he had encouraged you twice then you had another round for punishment.

I ran it easily, but there were classmates who almost succumbed. The last hundred meters you had to give your everything and you sprinted yourself empty. I did not turn my torso while running and therefore did not cut my breath away by every step and could usually still speed up the final meters.

Once stopped from the effort. You'd double up and you started to sweat like a pig. Then you had to walk around with your arms behind your head and breathe deeply. It is a miracle that we lived through it. The sweat was still in your eyes, and then he roared all: stretch em boys, stretching! He had a limited vocabulary and had standard commands that we had to follow. *Shower Time, last one in is a dead duck.* The showers were in a long line and sprayed cold water, so you almost had a stroke. The last one in, was the dead duck and had to dry mop the floor after showering.

After half a year I was fairly fluent in English. I had adapted well to my Texan schoolmates. I wore long pants, boots, and I drawled like a Texan. Everyone has his survival techniques. Now I learned that it was polite to begin a sentence with: May I, instead of Can I and eventually the differences between me and others disappeared. I learned that you had to ask: *may I go to the washroom*, if you meant toilet. I now read English pockets and I was back on the road of going to school with pleasure. I began to change, I became more self assured and I filled out and became strong. It was a gradual process, but one day it was just the way it was. I had become one of the bigger and stronger boys.

One of my bullies had not yet realized my change, he was not one of the brightest in his group, but he was very strong and tough. Without stopping, he sicked me all day. When he asked if he could go to the washroom, I asked a little later if I could go to the washroom as well. There he stood in front of a mirror putting brylcreme in his hair. 'Hey dickhead,' I said when I came in, 'you stink!'

Astonished, he turned around. 'Hey Dutchie are you talking to me, windmills forever ... hey..' I now repeated with more emphasis, boy, do you stink! He came to me and I did not wait, I gave him a great blow that blew him out of his shoes. All my frustrations of the past year was in that punch. *'Come on stinky'*, I invited him to get up, *'I will whip your ass'*. 'Oh, your friends are not here to help you, I said, 'that is too bad for you'. He grunted and came rushing at me and I gave him a second blow that made the blood run from his split lip and changed his nose into a fountain. Be sure you wash your hands after peeing, I advised him and walked out of the room.

It took a while before stinky came back, he had a piece of toilet paper crammed up his nostril to stop the bleeding.' Goh' said, Mr. Corcoran, who did not like foreign students and looked at me while he asked. 'what happened to you? 'I prepared myself to be sent away. But it is praise worthy of stinky, that he replied, I slipped. He immediately rose in my esteem. The bullying ceased after a day or two. I had become one of the boys. ***I am proud to be an American, protector of the poor, defender of freedom .***

Doebi game

Life in Tripoli for foreigners, took place in a few places. Your father worked, of course, so he went to the office and in the case of my father, he had several workstations. He worked at the main building of the Oasis Company, but a few times a month he flew out to the desert. The company had its own pipercubs and private pilots. Occasionally he went with some colleagues a little further than the normal concessions that they were at and he would go for a few days to Benghazi. The company was planning to build a floating pipeline a mile into the sea so the really big supertankers that could not enter the harbour could be filled from the shore. That took a lot of technology, technique that Libya and its natives did not have. The oil men from Texas were the most experienced people in the oil world. They came from the world of the famous Texan Adaire, the man who could extinguish burning oil wells. Those men and my father were true blood technicians and anything that seemed impossible but could be realized was like a challenge to them.

The company knew that, and pampered those men in cotton. Fathers had a bit of variety and spent their working time with peers. I went to school and the Oil Company was school five days a week and a part of my life. The same went for my brother, he studied at the Advanced College of Technology, a British / American Institute in Tripoli and the Arab students who were there admitted were of good families and differed in their way of life from the stone-throwing, not Muslim-hating mob. They came from countries like Syria or Lebanon, in order to attend the courses in Tripoli. They would become the first generation of well-trained Arab technicians.

Admission to the institute, was not to be laughed at. We were in the early 60s and in America, racial segregation had only been lifted in 1963 and riots and police protection of students of color admitted to "white" schools, had taken place, because new ideas take time to root. American society had to get used to the idea that people were equals. Such ideas drip down slowly. However, it was in the interest of the American oil companies in Libya to train young Arabs in technical subjects. At they end of the day they were required to have a certain percentage of Libyans on the payroll It is nice to know then that you are all singing from the same song book, or to think you are technically well formed and not simply added to on to the payroll. The people you had to adopt with no technical training were a danger to their technical environment. So up till then they had been paid for doing nothing.

My father and my brother and I still had a life outside of our house in Libya. My mother and my sisters absolutely did not have that luxury . My mother could only go to the *souk* (the market) when my brother and I went along shopping. During the day we were at school, she was "trapped" in the house. If my father was a weekend in the desert, we went with her while the sisters stayed at home. You took a horse taxi downtown and my mother was wrapped up in clothes, with a headscarf and even then you had to be careful that she would not be harassed. A woman on the street, a white woman, was offensive. As we walked along, it was clear that the woman who was walking with us was white under her clothes. If you did not walk along than she would certainly have been harassed because a woman alone should not be on the street. My sisters could not come along because my brother and I could not protect and my mother and my sisters If you saw an Arab walking with his wife then she followed him a few paces behind. Never would you see a couple walking arm in arm or hand in hand, that invited problems. In public there was no kissing that was contrary to good morals. Then you were at least fined. I guess it was not even lust or contempt of women, it was more an insult to our race. I can touch your wife. I dishonor your mother, your sister, I will block the road and grope her in passing. it is impossible to imagine such things, but it was the way it went. My mother's outings were on the side of my father, well packed in and with a headscarf. Or to worship on Wheelus Airbase on a Sunday, where you could just walk about freely. You come to realize the privileged position of Europeans and Americans in their respective countries. You appreciate your freedom really like a high good, if you've lived a time, in a backward country with a stone age mentality. We were hated and our women were despised and hated and desired.

When I came home from school, a cup of tea would be waiting for me and then I was allowed to play outside. That was allowed until dinner time, and after that I had to do my homework. There were a few Arab families who lived on the complex. Families with boys my age. They went to a French-Arabic school. With some French and some Arabic words we could make ourselves understood, that is if you'd accompany it with gestures where language failed. Playing tag bored quickly and we had invented a wonderful game. Muhammad Ali and his brother Abbat Misjier and me. We called the game *Doebi.* They were my friends in a way.

I cannot say it any different and we played with great fun with the little language that we had, to explain each other things. It had started when they had been looking at my little sisters who were playing in the garden with a swing. They were curious hanging over the fence. I was reading on the stairs next to the flowerbeds and I kept an eye on my sisters. When my sisters went inside I beckoned them and the garden one of the boys came hesitantly into the garden and sat down on the swing. The ice was quickly broken and we had a nice afternoon. It does not sound like very exciting, today with game boy toys, and so forth, but with almost no resources, we had really passed a nice time. They came from Egypt and their father did something for the government.

They taught me to count in Arabic and a kind of dice game where you keep stones behind your back and then you open hand simultaneously with that of your opponent and his bit wins or you lose your pebble. I lived in two worlds, in school with my American mates in a mini America and after school I lived in Libya in my garden. You could only do the rock or pebble gamble so often and and then you 'd get bored . That is why we invented the *Doebi* game I had a tennis ball and we started fiddling about. You would throw the ball over to your friend and the guys in the middle would have to catch the ball then change your place and you were the *lummel* , the one out.

Abbat taught me some words, he pointed out the trash barrel and said the Arabic word, a few stones that formed a English words, but because I was in the minority, the names remained predominantly Arabic. The rainpipe was called a doebi. Our game was a kind of baseball but without the bat because we didn´t have one. The pile of rocks, the garbage can and the rainpipe formed roughly three bases. Where the pitcher was standing served as the finishing point. The pitcher stood with his back to "the fi eld" back to front and one catcher stood in the middle. The pitcher threw the ball, trying to get that as high as possible in the air over his shoulder, and the catcher and the first runner meanwhile raced to a base. The catcher tried to hit him with the ball and if he did then the runner was out. With the four of you, it could not be played, we quickly learned from experience that you needed at least 8 to 10 players. Our means of communication were limited, but children get by as a rule with very little language. My friend Abbat, then came walking to the gate with some boys from his school and asked with raised eyebrows, Doebi? I took out the tennis ball and the next hour it was only screaming and laughing and running. It was a fun time. Abbat my best Arab friend, who taught me how to greet someone in Arabic. You would shake the left hand and with your right hand touch your heart and then your lips and forehead *yy Salam la likeem.* I feel no evil, hand on heart, I speak no evil, hand to your lips, I have no bad thoughts about you.. hand along your forehead. My American friends from Texas would have kicked my ass if they had seen me like that. Abbat my best Arabic friend, who in 1967 with a wild look in his eyes, would try to stone me.

Driving lessons:

Arab fellow students from my brother's school drove around in vw beetles. In a hot country it is an ideal car. Not because of its comfort, but by the fact that the beetles had air-cooled engines. They would never overheat, where water-cooled cars with a boiling radiator would come to a standstill, the vw's with their whistling screeching little boxer engine still merrily would run about The standard vws came with a 1100 cc engine. Young Arabs bought the top of the range, the 1200 cc or 1300 cc. Very occasionally you saw later a 1500 cc but those were such unprecedented heavy engines at that time that you had to be on a waiting list to obtain them. The young Arabs from affluent homes showcased wealth, they did not buy the monster, the 1500 cc vwt nor the cheapest entry-level version, the 1100 cc, usually they tore around in the 1200 cc and 1300 cc versions.

'Pimp up', the word did not exist, but if it had existed it would have been a good way to describe those cars they were all pimped up. Not to impress women or young girls, because they were not there, not to outdo each other and stab eyes out. Glitter, glitter, chrome exhausts, and spaghetti exhaust pipes which converted those whistling tones and squeaking sounds into a deep baritone. The radio was also adamant turned on, so everyone heard you had a radio. Cassette tapes did not exist and if they had existed then all my brother's Arabic friends who certainly have had them.

My brother had a great time at the Technical College. The teachers were Americans or Englishmen, and it was clear you had to throw the hat to your studies not to pass the exams as a white man. I will say that there was a strong preference. A policy that favoured those of the same tribe.. The Arab students were impeccably dressed in a Western way. Suit and tie. They came from Lebanon and from Syria and from neighboring Egypt. Countries which were then seen, in the Arab world, as examples of civilization.

They were modern and prosperous and would like Ataturk, a century before them in Turkey, participate in a modern world based on Western ideals. There were no Turkish students because Turkye had themselves universities and educational institutes. You might wonder why the Lebanese and Syrians did not go to their neighbor Turkye, to study? Because they realized that after finishing the "advanced College of Technology", which was co-founded by the American oil companies employment would almost happen seamlessly in those same companies.

Why would the Oasis oil company have an application round far away on the other side of the Mediterranean sea, in Turkye, if they could draw them from their own technical pond, recommended to them by teachers from our their own stock to offer them a job. The foreign Arab students looked down on the Libyans, which they regarded as pathetic uneducated retarded morons. That was eyopener to me, when my brother once invited a couple of his friends to our home. I could never have imagined that there was discrimination among the Arabs.

They were polite with good manners and it hurts to know now, that their countries will not be in gear with modern civilization, but that as we know now, looking back to the years that followed, slipped back into feudal civil war-like conflicts, which must have been devastating to the early ideals cherished by the fellow students from my brother's institute. They came roaring down our lane with their beetles and parked outside our house. The boys drank coca cola as a pinnacle of American integration and averted their eyes when my sister walked past. They were more civilized than many Texan oil father I knew, but that was easy. The Texan men had been at their posts for years and regarded the world as their oyster.

My brother was invited by two brothers students for a return visit to Lebanon, to which he adhered the following summer and he came back with descriptions of beautiful cities, wealth and civilization and a gift for me, a dagger with the inscription, Welcome to Lebanon. He was treated and adopted as a brother. They wanted in those circles to be in touch with white foreigners, than they rose in status. As it would be in Western countries, much later, to have in your circle of friends a colored person, which was seen as politically correct. Later my brother was the white negro in Lebanese circles. He was exhibited everywhere by the father of the brothers as a sign of success, that his own sons enjoyed in Libya. His sons had European friends.

They had a distorted picture of Israel and America's role in it. They idolized German engineering and knew of Rommel and his desert rats that had been VW like vehicles passing up and down the desert fighting. The coin fell. They wanted America's or European's aid because in engineering in Libya, they ruled the roost, but had a lot of respect for the holocaust against their arch enemies, the Israelites caused by the Germans. They had a confused picture about the war and how it had happened. I assume your view of history is determined by where you learn about it. In Germany, the 2nd World War will be discussed differently from Japan, or in England or America.

In our country 70 years after the war, the Germans, are still regarded and referred to as pigs by some groups, tolerance is still far out of reach with the new generation which is far removed from the actual war. Let alone in the 60's, years when my brother's Arab friends at the time, were only years from the Holocaust, 15 years removed from the German triumphs, and 15 years of the creation of Israel by Americans and British, by giving Palestine to their archenemies, a new country by the Americans and the British. In particular, the formation of the Israeli state was confusing for them and the role of the countries in it, with which they would love to collaborate with. America and Europe. Fair is fair, I suppose that most of us find it confusing, and given that, the Americans and British must have scratched themselves behind the ears at times.

My father heard a thing or two and did not interfere in the political discussions that are so part of student life. Together with my brother, he was a good host. After one of these meals, when the beetles were waved out, he asked my brother, 'would you not like to have such a beetle?' My brother asked, *really*, in disbelief? 'Yes', said my father, who had developed, after sharing his office for many years with the Texans, racist tendencies. 'If those niggers can get a car, why can't you'? I had often noticed, my father found anything that was not white, a Negro. Most likely that was caused by his childhood in Java and fueled by Texans where, even today, the Klux klux clan still have roots. I could not put my finger on it, but it was ugly and unnecessary. Arabs are no niggers. Negroes are not Arabs. Whites are neither and we can still go on for a while with definitions. People are people with equal rights, but not always equal. A generalization like this, which my father so often committed with respect to races, was a first step towards separation between him and me a few years later, when the hippie era shot root in full force.

'Well', said my father. 'You have to get your license first'. If you pass your test I'll buy you a beetle'. I could hardly believe my ears.' But a nice beetle said my father, one that stands out a bit'. After class, I'll immediately start looking for a driving school, said my brother. When my father was flown the next day for a week to the desert, my brother came home, much later than usual.' I went to a driving school', he explained.' With one of my student friends,' 'Gee,' I said.' Yes,' my brother said, 'it is an Egyptian instructor, a relative of his. He speaks a little English."Oh, that's convenient', I thought. 'Tomorrow after school I'll start and next week and I'll drive off'. 'Impressive,' I said.

'Mechemet's school,' said my brother,' they guarantee that you pass.' 'Can they do that,' I asked, it seems quite complicated to me.' 'I have to ask mom for some money', my brother said,' because you pay per lesson.' I did not have enough with me otherwise I would have already had my first lesson. In a country where nothing happens, these are interesting developments and I waited impatiently for my brother's return home the next day. He came home a bit later and beamed. 'Tell me,' I said, 'how did it go?' 'Very well,' my brother said, 'Mechemet is very satisfied.' 'What did you have to do,' I wanted to know from my big brother, who in my eyes was almost a man now.

'We drove around a bit', said my brother 'and I had to repeat things.' 'What do you see?' 'Then he took a turn, he put an indicator signal on and went around the bend. Then he parked the car and said again *lookie please* !, and then he turned the engine off and then he turned the key a bit, and then he started the car again.

'He drove', I said in disbelief,' but you must learn to drive! 'That comes naturally,' says mr Mechemet. 'Tomorrow we'll go on.' 'Oh okay,' I said, 'because I understood that Mr. Mechemet really knew what he was doing.' What kind of car are you driving in,' I asked. 'A beetle,' said my brother. 'That's handy,' I said, 'because that is what Pa is getting you. Nice going man!' The next day my brother could shift gears. 'There are four gears,' my brother told me, it is a type H shift. I listened in awe. 'Left upper H is first gear and below the second, and the third is in the upper right leg and the fourth below'. My brother had become a technical genius in my eyes. 'Did you go really fast', I asked? 'No,' my brother said,' we were standing still'. I had to dry shift without moving. I understood that the beetle of mr Mechemet would never wear out. 'There are three pedals,' my brother carried on, with the right pedal you give gas, you do that with your right foot. In the middle is the brake, which you control with your right foot and the left pedal is used when you want to change to another gear.

Eventually the Saturday came that my brother would go for his driver's test. That same afternoon he came home beaming with pride and joy. He held out a piece of paper in his hand.' I made it,' he laughed. 'Dude,' I shouted,' that is fantastic may I see it?' 'This is a provisional license a kind of statement', he said,' the final one comes within two weeks. 'Gosh,'was it hard,' I asked? 'Well no man,' replied my brother,' I had to pay £ 20 exam fee and mr Mechemet, sat beside me in the car.' 'I had to control all the buttons and dry shift'. 'Yes,' I said expectantly. 'Then I had to start the car. That went well and then I had to do it all again. Mr. Mechemet was very satisfied and said, *yes yes, you good* .. and then I got this statement.

My father looked crestfallen when he saw the statement, but he kept his word, and on Monday my brother and I went with my father to look at the VW showroom. There were two military drab-colored beetles, green poo color. My father ordered him the color he wanted, a cream-colored white one, he would have to have some patience because it had to come from far away. At home, my father got out of his car and looked at my brother proudly.

'Park it under the tree,' he said. My brother looked really weird when he sat down behind the wheel. My father's car was different, he had an Opel Captain which had a column gear shift. 'You first gear is up towards you,' dictated my father. The car stalled four times when my brother led the clutch come up. Fair to say that with the last attempt the car did hop forward a little before it stalled. 'Right', said my father, is mr Mechemet a berber?

Dangerous jars

My brother had been working for some time in the garden and that surprised me. My brother read a lot and that made me feel comfortable because that meant I had reading material as well, but actively working in the garden, was something that did not suit him. After a while he walked out of our garden and disappeared along the side of the communal parking. Occasionally he stopped and he lifted up some rocks. I watched him until he disappeared around the corner and out of sight. I was reading. Houses in Libya are slightly raised above a sort of poured concrete slab and I was reading on the these steps leading up to the slab. As a result, you automatically get a raised deck around your house. You can then safely walk around you home. Hot countries always bring about nasty animals.

I always sat on the three steps leading up to the circulation, reading. It was my favorite place. Because of its location it was a relatively cool spot and the cold tiles were pleasant to sit on. You sat near the back door. You could put away your book and with a few steps you were in the kitchen where you could take a drink, then again to return to the laid down adventures of my brother's preference in reading material .. Books were hard to get by in a country that was highly illiterate and which also used a different script with a lot of tricks and curls. Europe is very set on the written word, you will find magazines or books in which ever supermarket and in many grocery stores.

In Tripoli there were no supermarkets. There were shops where they sold some bread and cans and vegetables and then you had had it. No Arabic magazines were sold, let alone that they would cater for the hated foreigners. Our part of the world is so incredibly luxurious in comparison, there is no comparison. My brother and I read mostly English books and I depended on his preference.

My father had subscribed to Time magazine and the National Geographic magazine, which he received at his office and if they had gone through many collegiate hands they ended up with some delay under our coffee table in neat piles. In the April issue there had been a fascinating article about scorpions, my brother and I had read it several times. Just because it joined into a part of our reality, of our own lives in Libya which was full of scorpions.

You might read in June, the Time of April, but that did not matter, in a country that is cut off from civilization as we knew, every page about that civilization had news value. I had the misfortune of depending on what my brother went for, strong thematic reading. He bought or swapped books with American classmates who brought them back at the American Airbase, where we came on Sundays at Wheelus airbase to attend a church service.

We had a pass that only gave us permission to enter the airbase on Sundays. Americans had freer access to the base. So at a young age I came into contact with the Superhero magazines such as Superman, Captain America or Gi. Joe, what a twisted view it gave us about how the world war was won by the actions of many brave GI's. Invariably with a few German words in it, in order to boost a reality setting. The few Germans in it, always had names like, *Hans, Heinz, Claus or Fritz*, it occurred, and none of them had wanted the war. They shouted *Achtung* and *lieber Gott* and shot their *Snauzer*s empty on the heroes who came to liberate Europe.

If you had read ten of them, then you could write the next one yourself. I regretted my brother's taste. But where there is not, the Emperor loses his right. He had times when he was obsessed with cowboy stories, I could not do anything with it, I found those, incredibly stupid macho stories. From my studies, later in life I would learn that they were all "flat characters", who played the main roles. There was one exception, in my view, on the whole and that was the cycle of Winnetou, the Indian chief. We had two Dutch parts of it,, that did not join up. *Hauw,* I still do not know what happened to the pale faces and their forked tongue ... and when I found myself in areas years later able to gain that knowledge, my age had passed the interest level of Winnitou, *hauw.*

Mr. Harper had at school a bookshelf and in the pause during his presence you could read from there, the downside was that you were stuck with many interrupted stories My mother's book club sent no books to Libya and the few books she had brought, I had read. In Libya there was nothing to read! While the whole world enjoyed Zorba the Greek, outside Libya we remained deprived of even movie theaters or movies. What poor wretch in Libya would go to a movie and then only be confronted with images of luxury that they would never reach. Where streets were filled on the screen with cars and women in jeans who also drove cars and even fulfilled hero roles. There was an old theater of the Italian colonial period, which showed films where everything was dubbed over in Arabic, because there is so much illiteracy in Libya and who could read subtitles?

We had to amuse themselves. During the day we were at school, but when the school doors shut behind you and you walked to your house then you were back in that other world. The world that had a lot to catch up, which was driven by fanaticism and hatred. Rudyard Kipling said it in one of his earlier poems, **East is east and West is West and never the twain Shall meet ..** It's sad but I have to agree with him. Other worlds with completely different ideas. Just like a Venn diagram in mathematics, with two circles that partly overlap, creating a shaded area indicating the common collection , so we were with the Libyans, as exponents of a larger underlying collection gathered at the point where the collections overwrite each other. But with very little in common. If one is in the red portion then it was still possible to count on a certain degree of tolerance, but again with the laws in force of the underlying habits outside that area.

My brother came in sight and saw me watching him. He beckoned me and when I came near, he asked, 'get me some empty glass jars from the kitchen, we are going hunting'. 'What do you mean jars and we are going hunting,' I wanted to know? 'Get them now, and you can help me'. I came back with four pots. 'We are going to catch scorpions,' said my brother. 'Oh', I said 'why?' 'To take care of and study' he explained, 'if we had enough we can give them to my Arab friends who will fry them.' I had seen those kind of snacks, fried seahorses and scorpions. It seemed like a great plan. So an old April issue of National Geographic still proved useful.

From the article we knew that scorpions had 12 eyes, spread all over their body. Had no angel, but a stinger on aspine lump and were poisonous. That they made a soft raspy sound with their feet before attacking,such a sound as we would never be able to observe and that they would rather flee, then attack. I wondered whether the National Geographic writer had caught scorpions himself and whether it was true that they exhibited escape behavior. 'A child can do the laundry,' my brother said. 'We want different types and we cannot put them together in a jar, because they are cannibalistic in nature', 'I have found eight of the buggers', he stated proudly. We knew the article by heart and I knew something like 8 finding places on a few Square metres was not impossible. Under rocks, they crop up, they dig themselves into voids and spaces, in short, with the National Geographic in hand, the devilish spawn had no chance. We walked to the first location, a long flat stone. 'How do we get them' I asked. 'If you do it right,' my brother said, 'grab them by the poisonous stinger with a pair of tweezers, but you have to handle them with care, otherwise you'll damage them. I hoped that scorpions would just display just as much concern for our well being. 'For reasons of clarity', I said,' I will kick the stone away and you can pick it up.' 'Well no,' said my brother, I will hold the jar down and you lower the critter in there.

'I do not think so', I said, 'no way!' 'What are you, a coward,' my brother said. 'Ok,' I said, 'I'll do it, but then you do it first, just to show me how'. 'No I can't' said my brother because I am holding the jar.' 'I'll just go back to reading again,' I answered and made as if to walk away. 'Hold on,' my brother said, 'I have a twig, we wil put the jar down and drive with a stick the scorpion in the jar. Then you put the lid on it'. I found that acceptable. It was a good plan. You took a stone away and stirred with a stick in the sand around the scorpion which made no sound whatsoever, nor showed any flight behavior and drove him to the jar while his tail with the poison stinger furiously hit from left to right. The glass jar gave them no hold and you put it upright quickly and you screwed the lid on. My brother used his pocketknife for some air holes in the lid and number one was trapped.

Looking back I now know that we had tackled immediately one of the most toxic types , whose poison equalled that of the deadly cobra.The five stripe scorpion is extremely deadly. He was not to be found in the National Geographic article. The four jars were filled quickly and we took them home. 'I think Mom does not need to know', said my brother and I understood him, women simply react differently to scorpions' than the hunters do, that have entangled them. My brother and I shared a bedroom and there under his bed our little friends found their place. Closer to your master you could not be.

They remained wonderfully alive, my brother took them locusts and pieces of meat and trickled occasional water inside. Our collection, which after a few weeks had become a true strain of scorpions 14 total, we had beautiful translucent, black, smaller specimens, was discovered at a time when we were in school. My mother was apoplectic when she wanted to sweep under the bed. There stood jar after jar of scorpions. When we got home we knew something was wrong. 'Sit down,' said my mother, who has brought the vermin in to my house?' 'If you are talking about the scorpions,' my brother,' replied, 'us', pointing to both of us, by moving his index finger back and forth between us.

'Why,' my mother asked, startled? 'They do not do anything', answered my brother. 'I do not want them in my house,' my mother said firmly.' Well then we will clean them up', said my brother. 'I've already done so', my mother replied, 'I had Muhammad remove them.' Have you got anymore critters stashed away in my house,' she asked?' 'No,' we said, and we saw for our mental eye how Muhammad sat at the table with our friends, fried and all and eating them with great pleasure.

The base

'If any of you guys want to come, you can,' my father said. He looked at my brother and me after the invitation. It was about a short stay in the desert over the weekend. My father had to be contractually present at some new work. 'You can't come both', my father said, 'One of you must stay home to protect the women.' That sounded already pretty Arabic, but we understood him. 'We'll fly out Friday and come back Sunday afternoon.' 'However, bring a rain jacket with you, because it may well rain." Rain,' we asked surprised?' In the desert?' 'That is what they say in the office,' my father replied. Americans were always very well informed, but this seemed to us both unimaginable. There was not a cloud in the sky, everything was 'clear blue sky.

'It's two hours away, which is not much in time but in distance it is', continued my father. 'In the night it freezes even where we are.' 'There is a big difference between day and night temperatures.' I realized that I knew very little about my father's work and his working conditions. He just left home and came back home and I had never wondered what it would be like in the wilderness. 'I would really like hat,' I said, and my brother said,' it does not matter to me' and that made me the chosen one.

Oasis Oil company was one of the largest producers of oil in Libya. It was a company that consisted of a few companies from Texas and there was no end to the money. I had once heard my father talking with colleagues, but the numbers had meant nothing to me then. Now in retrospect they do. They produced 300 000 barrels of oil per day and had several concessions. Those concessions were awarded by the government for a period of five years. After that, part of those concessions fell back to the Libyan government. I later realized, that this was to encourage rapid exploration and "mine" new fields. The government received 25% of tax on each barrel produced. In addition, the companies were forced to have a percentage of Arabic personnel on the payroll.

Oil people with the "know-how" were of the greatest importance for the major companies. The major contributors were the geologists and engineers. 'John Tidwell also flies with us,' my father said. Mr. Tidwell had no children and had agreed to act as our guardian if something were to happen to my parents. It was a nice, quiet man who sometimes came to have dinner at our home with us and it was one of the geologists of the company. 'What are you going to check,' I asked my father? I want to take some samples and they are going to pour a base and I want to be there. 'A base,' I asked surprised? I only knew Wheelus air base. 'A foundation base,' continued my father, ' we will assemble a new complex on it". Oh,'

I said, not realizing that I would be witnessing a day later an incredible technical operation. The vans of the company came along after lunch and my father and I got on board. There were quite a few people in the van. We only had one bag for the two of us with us, but there were people with a suitcase, They probably stayed out a little longer, I estimated.

' So Dan', someone said to my father, 'is that your son?' 'Yeah',said my father. 'Looks like a fi ne boy to me', the man was done with me, I was dismissed because he was now discussing matters that went over my head. All technical stuff. Typical Texas talk, someone is a fine boy. I looked a bit out of the window and we came to an airstrip. The company itself had some planes. The van drove to the larger type aircraft, I believe it was a Beechcraft, you could have 6 people in and fit quite some baggage. There were also pipercubs but they were significantly smaller.

We hopped in and a man in a T-shirt and khaki pants came up last. 'Hi Bill' it sounded from all sides. Bill was the pilot.' Hi Folks', Bill replied, and it dawned on me again that everything and everyone was American. Bill sat down, checked some clocks and gauges, fiddled with some switches and put his thumb up. There came a man from a barrack with a giant battery on wheels, and a moment later the two propeller engines came alive. Bill let the left and then the right control fl ps go up and down and was apparently satisfied. 'Okay folks', he called over his shoulder, 'we are ready'. He taxied to an airstrip, took a good look around, 'Roger', he said in the radio,' all systems go' and he opened the throttle. We bounced twice off and then bounced into the air. 'So,' my father said to a colleague, 'Bill is getting better.' We were not flying high and the landscape that unfolded was a large expanse of sand. The continuous whirring drone of the engines meant that talks were impossible. Most oilboys sat with their eyes closed, some dozing. After about two hours of flying Bill drew a sharp turn that pushed us half off our chair and gave us a view of a complex which we circled around. There were even there some small planes and some sheds and kind of barrack-like caravans. 'Is this guy really a pilot', I asked my father? 'Oh, yeah', replied my father,' he is one of the better pilots. A cowboy, huh?' 'They are too old for the Air Force and then go in to civilian flying.' Bill came hurtling down hard and probably thought he was in fighter jet. He pulled the plane up just above the ground and with a bang and some bouncy jumps we landed at concession 52.

Mr. Tidwell and my dad had their own accommodation with air conditioning, a shower and some bunk beds. I had not expected to find airconditioning in the desert. There was a large hangar-like Romney hall, with a buffet bar. The men were given free food and drinks, but there was no alcohol and taking it along from Tripoli or consuming alcohol inevitably led to dismissal. You could just walk in and take whatever you wanted. The chefs worked just like the other men 24 hours around the clock in shifts. My father was a moment later outside with drawings under his arm and looked around outside, at the steel braid.

A large Caterpillar, with steel tracks shoved, what seemed to be, a level road until very far away, through the sand. The loose sand hid a bedrock hard layer. I sat with Mr. Tidwel behind a coke and we looked at the Caterpillar going to and fro levelling the trajectory of the road. How did they get a caterpillar, I was wondered, we were really in the middle of nowhere.

'What is that guy doing', Mr. Tidwell, I asked? 'Oh, he is preparing a runway', he said. 'Have you come along for this project', I asked?' Well no', he said,' tomorrow I go with a few men deeper into the desert to an interesting place. I have a few days off and I'm going to practice my hobby.' 'Your hobby', I asked politely? 'Geology', smiled, Mr. Tidwell. 'I will go to a petrified forest.. and our conversation stopped because my father came in. 'Okay', he said,' he probably will never see in his life again, what's is about to happen. We are ready to do go.' 'You have to promise me that you stay inside.' The Caterpillar was gone and the track looked very good.

Even in the Romney hangar, we could hear the deep rumble of very heavy airplane engines come nearer. There appeared a dot in the sky that quickly grew and I saw one of the most incredible large military aircraft I had ever seen coming in for a landing. it landed on the runway that the caterpillar had just pushed and only came to a stop at the end. The engines continued to run and the machine turned to be able to take off again. A huge tailgate was lowered and not to be believed a cement truck with rotating drum came driving out. The door closed again and the plane engines revved up, the brakes were thrown off and the big green bird was back in the air. The concrete truck was driving on instructions of a foreman to the braid, where Arabs with boots and a vibrating plate were ready to vibrate air bubbles out of the 'pour' and to make the whole into a nice flat slab of concrete.

The driver came in for a coke and gulped that quickly away when the next plane drone announced itself. The same kind of giant landed, lowered the tailgate and a concrete truck came driving out after which the first driver drove his empty truck inside. The plane took off and had been no more than five minutes on the ground. American effiency in top gear. I assumed that the planes came flying in from Wheelus Airbase. My father explained that they had chosen for the concrete pour at the end of the afternoon, because in the hot sun, the concrete dries quickly and cracks. 'Two more planes I would say', my father said, and looked anxiously at the sky which began to go overcast. Another team Arabs now sprayed with a hose the first 'pour' wet and when they had come to the end then they turned around and came walking up and hosing again.. The last plane had just taken the empty concrete truck and was loose when the first drops began to fall. It started to rain, not just a shower, but a torrential waterfall of rain. 'Hey', I said. 'those Arabs are still hosing the pour down.' 'I know.' my father said. Their long dresses clung to their bodies while we, with a coke in hand, followed the operations from behind the glass wall, 'Why do you not stop them'. 'No, boy', my father said, 'you have much to learn.' You should never confuse Arabs. We have said that they have to hose everything down and they do so without realizing why. If we stop them now we seem to be saying contradictory things. 'Then next time, when if it is not raining, with such a job, they might not take us serious. No, if we tell them to hose a concrete slab down for a few hours, then that is what they do.'. That gave me a different perspective on things. Now the rain drummed hard rhythms on the steel roof of the shed and the water ran from the hair and the clothes of the men outside who stood there dunking in their boots.

Trees made of stone:

In the evening, the rain stopped as suddenly as it had begun. Big spotlights illuminated the concrete slab and another shift of Arabs team cleaned the hoses up. The whole complex was brightly lit. We sat in the Romney shed and the men drank some pop drinks before going to bed. Groups of men talking at tables about the work of the next shift and a lot were reading magazines. Others played games. There were no movies or tv's and the video recorder had yet to be invented. At once it struck me, even though you saw Arabs all day, who sat together in groups and doing tedious jobs, I had not seen the whole afternoon and evening an Arab in Romney shed.

'Should the other men not eat', I asked my father and John Tidwell? 'What do you mean, what other men,' asked John? 'Well the Arabs, we just saw at work,' I replied. 'The Mo's,' he asked and raised his eyebrow? Well I looked surprised. 'The *Mo's*,' said John,' eat separately, that is better for them and for us.' I was so innocent that I thought they all came from the Mo tribe. We were in the desert with mainly people from Texas, a southern state in America, in the early 60s. The time that America drastically separated races in their own country, under the name of segregation.

'Why do you call them Mo's,' I started? 'Oh', John laughed,'because of their prophet Mohammed'.' They all have weird names, so if we need one, than we shout Muhammad and then there is always one that comes running. I understood that these were Arabs who were obligatory on the payroll. John, who knew so much and had studied so much called every Arab, a Mo, because it was too much trouble for him to remember their names. The "Mo's" in Tripoli also had their families and those were proud of their in the wilderness working fathers, who worked for an American multinational 2 months in the desert and then earned in those two months more than their relatives in a year.

I now know what the difference was between these pragmatic technicians and experts and me. I can give it a name. They had no empathy. They could not move in the lives of the 'Mo's', they were just annoying people that you got assigned to the payroll.' Look young Daniel,' John said, they cannot eat certain things because of their faith, and they would not feel at ease with us. The food preparation, I understood, that was a good argument. and the rest seemed nonsensical. You cannot explain anything to them,' John went on, they can quard and clean up a bit and that is it. You may never give them the work of a white man, it would go wrong. 'They are negroes, but of the worst kind'.

I asked myself seriously if anyone had ever tried to explain anything to the Mo's. I suspected that I already knew the answer, no! 'There are many people with different possibilities in society', John lectured on' In the States, it is important that you have had a good education if you want to live comfortably. ' You cannot see from a distance if a white man has had a proper training , whether he is prepared to deliver high performance.' 'That's pleasant with Mo's you can see from a distance who they are..You recognize them with their deficits'. I understood that I could not voice my thoughts yet into words yet and let it go past me. 'Where do they sleep,' I asked? 'In tents,' my father replied, they find that enjoyable.' I began to understand why the Arabs did not like us. The arrogance of the white society that ruthlessly ruled the roost. I will take a few shoot Mo's along tomorrow with me', John continued. I began to understand it was not meant bad, it was the time spirit speaking through the mouths of those men who were superior in that particular circumstance.

'Are you not afraid that the guards turn may against you, they have guns and you do not,' I asked.' Oh no' another Texan joined in, a man who would die badly burned a few months later thanks to a "Mo"', they are very happy with us and they kiss the whip. They listen to authority and respect us'. 'The mo's,' he continued, only have awe for power. My father could only identify the men months later burned, beside the exploded plants by their ornate cowboy boots.

'What do you need the Mo's for,' asked my father? 'I am going to the petrified forest to collect fossils' answered my later guardian. 'We will take one of the rat mobiles and I want two shooting Mo's along, you never know what you encounter'. The Germans called General Rommel, as a name of honor, desert fox, the Americans called the same German hero who was fighting pulled back and forth through the desert in vw like vehicles, the desert rat. The company had dune buggy-like vehicles with wide tires that had air-cooled VW engines thus these were called ratmobiles. The world war had come to an end 15 years earlier All wounds were still fresh.

'Gosh', I said, 'a petrified forest, really?''Certainly young Daniel,' said John, 'would you like that?' I looked at my father, 'if you like, he said, I'm comfortable with it. It's not far from here and we will not fly until tomorrow, Sunday'. Wow, this was fun, infinitely more fun than reading my brother's paperback on my stairs in the garden That night I lay in my bunk and let everything again pass in review. The flight from Tripoli to concession 52, I had already found an adventure. I had a better idea of my father's work, at least now I had a picture, the heavy transport aircraft had been most impressive.

The last part of a conversation between my father and his collegial friend that night, went over air and space. The conversations were always of technical or scientific nature. Concession 52 was a heaven for technicians, they could talk about their passion, in all its forms and manifestations, with kindred spirits who understood them instantaneously. At home no one could talk about his work. It were separate worlds. John, I remember, said to my father; 'within 10 years we will put a man on the man.' He was wrong, it happened eight years later.' I should be very wrong if we did not have a moon base before 2000 and realize a fl ight to Mars, he continued. Again, he was wrong, but that was more due to the shifting of political beacons and austerity measures at NASA. I slipped into a deep sleep filled with Mo's, petrifi ed forests and moon landings. In the morning we enjoyed a hearty breakfast in the Romney shed.' I asked the cook to prepare packed lunches,' reported mr Tidwell while he took a sip of juice. 'You should drink enough' he advised me, 'you will lose moisture soon enough'. The cook came out with a bag with the name tag: ***young Daniel***, on it, and I knew that nothing was left to chance. Moments later we were at the workshop of concession 52, mechanics were tinkering with cars and there was a row of buggies ready to be used. 'Right,' said the chief mechanic with a heavy Texan accent, 'where does the journey take you, gentlemen?' 'The Petrified Forest', said John and the mechanic shook his head pityingly. 'You have to want to do it, 50 + degrees at least today, are you looking for something in particular?' 'The usual, arrowheads and fossils, that sort of thing,' said Mr. Tidwell, 'and I want to teach young Daniel some geological principles'.

'Enjoy it', the man wished us,' I have the ***"lady be good"*** for you ready and refueled. The lady be good, it read on the side of the buggy. The man filled in a sheet and wrote next to it, the date and: Tidwell and assistant and petrified forest. 'Then we know where to look if you do not come back', he smiled at me. Again it dawned on me how professional everything was done here. 'Not to control you,' John said, 'but just in case', he opened the glove box compartment and said, 'compass,' 'check' said the mechanic and ticked something off a list. 'Injection kit and antidote serum,' 'check' said the mechanic, 'extra water and flare gun,' 'check' said the mechanic.

'Nice, now we must pick some Mo's up and then we'll go for it,' John was excited and so was I. It was obvious when you mocked the desert then things would go bad for you, just as it had for the original crew of the **Lady be good,** a B24 bomber that had flown off course in the war on a wrong compass reading . The aircraft had flown past the base and the crew thought that they'd f nd the base on sight, but in reality they were flying every minute further away from the base until the fuel was gone and they had crashed into the desert. The crew had survived the crash and tried to reach the base on foot. However, they were still with the wrong coordinates of their compass and walked toiling miles further , deeper and deeper into the desert. Had they just shot sun, by determining together with their watch, the angle of the sun than they had known that the base was behind them and not in front of them. They are such trifles that are fatal. They had dehydrated and were found 15 years later. The plane still had air in the tires and was left where it had landed.

Our Lady be good started immediately and John slapped the seat next to him, 'Oh where, oh were could my student geologist be,' he shouted?' 'Come on boy, hop in the car'. And so I did.' Now we were on our way!' The car jumped forward direction checkpoint. There was the head of the security service. John stopped the car. 'So mr Tidwel are you going on research', smiled the man? 'Almost', replied John,' I still need some Mo's, have you got two shooting niggers for me?' 'Preferences,' the man asked? 'No, 'John said.' Hey you,' called the head of security out, to a few men with their backs leaning against the checkpoint in the shade with their rifles between their knees, he whistled and pointed with his thumb to the empty seat of the lady be good. The men got up slowly and now we scampered away.

It was hot and the air quivered and seemed to wave in the distance and turn it into a liquid mirror of water. 'What do you know of petrified wood' John asked. 'Nothing,' I answered, 'until yesterday I had never heard of it.' 'Has the wood then really become rock?' 'Oh yeah,'John said, I'll tell you a bit about it then you appreciate it more, later. Libya has not always been primarily desert', started my mentor. 'You can actually only talk about Libya in a certain time area. Now in this era, today it is a dry desert, but just imagine that 29 million years ago, where we travel here, it was a tropical area with inland seas'. 'Was this sea then', I asked? 'Yes,' said John. 'Do you know how oil is created, the crude oil?' I did have a bit of an idea. 'Through putrefaction,' I replied, 'organic residues under high pressure turns into oil in marshes, I believe.' 'That's close', said my future guardian.' 'You need to actually talk about fossil fuels'. 'Coal and lignite are formed by swampy conditions, you're right there. Crude oil, crude oil, is another story, a story that is separate from swamps.' Where we are going today, was a site with swamp like conditions and therefore it is a site of fossils and petrified wood.'

'Where are we driving now, was seabed, which is important for the formation of oil.' 'The preliminary phase of oil is something that you call earth wax or kerogen. This only occurs when a sediment layer forms on the seabed.' 'Oh', I said, how was it that a stranger explained to me in a few words how oil was formed and that my father and I had never talked about it? My father, who had worked all his life in the oil business.

'On the condition, however', John said, 'that the sea floor was oxygen poor. Then the organic radicals are devoured due to partial decomposition and form the kerogen, and if, after a period of time and again we are talking about a long-time plane, sediment deposits on those residues come to pass, then they are transformed under pressure into a chemical composition. It is then transformed into crude oil.' Oh,' I said again to show that I listened closely. 'Only one more thing missing to my story,' John continued,' the conversion process takes place only at a temperature of 100 degrees or more'. 'But you soon reach that when you come deeper in the earth's crust. Ideal conditions are oil reserves between 2 and 4 miles deep. The temperature prevailing there is a constant of 80 to 100 degrees'.

'Well', I said, I never knew that. 'You do not need to know' John continued, 'this only builds on your understanding of your surroundings.' ' Does oil float on water,' asked John? 'Yes', I said, I knew that from school, 'to a thickness of spreading of one molecule'. 'Okay,' said my mentor 'and what is lighter oil or gas?" Gas,' I promptly replied. 'Therefore,' John said, 'you always will drill first through a layer of gas and we f are that off, then you reach the oil layer and below that you have the water layer'. 'I look for conditions that hold the promise of oil within themselves, and if I can find those, and we do a test drilling, then we have water immediately. Even if you are ever so far into the desert.' That was news to me.' Under very Libya,' continued John,' you have underground seas, rivers and lakes. That goes for most of Africa,' he concluded.

We had been driving for a while and I let the newly acquired knowledge sink in to me. Now the road started to rise and I understood that we were indeed driving over an ancient sea floor to a higher plateau. I tried to set it to a landscape with tropical trees, and dinosaurs or elongated fields of waving crops. The increase was very gradual but noticeable.' Here it begins the said John, but we'll carry on and then we will arrive at the trees.

So we drove a bit later on a plain with incredible petrified trees in all shapes and sizes. The cross-sections of some trees were considerably enormous. They lay in chunks, large stone chunks with the petrified drawing of the bark and with visible growth rings in the sun. 'So,' said my mentor, when he pulled the car to the side, 'first drink a bit or we will end up poorly.' We continued down and drank a can of soda. The Arabs took a swig from their canteen. Then we got out while the two men kept sitting in the car. The benefit of the heat was compared to Tripoli, that there were not flies here. Such details hit you after a time. John said, 'you know, hey, you want to pick something up, you kick against it first. It seems strange but here you'll f nd multitudes of scorpions under the stones.

I wanted to take a piece of a tree, but stone weighs more than wood and I eventually had to settle for a small branch that I could handle but which still weighed plenty. I walked to the car and put it in there, the Arabs looked at me stoically. John ran here and there looking about and picked up some pebbles. 'Come and have a look', he said, 'you know what these are?' He held some pebbles in his hand. 'Yes, they are stones,' I said. 'This,' said John, 'is f int, fl int has a hardness of 7 on a scale of 1 to 10, you take a good look at it, what do you see? I looked and suddenly I saw it, they were all pointed, but not only that, they had been edited. Incidentally, you can pick up a pebble with pointed ends, but if you pick a selective 5 stones that are all pointed on one side, then you go look at them in more detail. 'These are arrowheads,' explained John. 'The area is full of concretions, formations of flint' 'You can see that they have been edited. If you hit hard on flint you get a fracture surface with sharp edges, which is due to the stress wave in the rock by the stroke on it'.

'People have made arrowheads here from pieces of stone, through editing.' 'Gosh, how old is that do you think,' I asked. 'That is a problem with stone objects,' said John, 'the points are from the stone age and that ran from 2 million years ago to 10 000 years ago. It is more important to me that people once have lived here'.

We walked back and ate some in the car and took another drink, Then we drove a little further, deeper into the forest.' How do you think wood turns to stone,' asked my mentor? 'I was just about to ask that,' I said. 'What do you think,' he asked? 'Under high pressure, maybe, I would not know'. 'Here has been a swamp,' said John, 'and the trees or other fossils that we encounter have fallen in that swamp'. 'It may also have been a muddy field, and not necessarily a swamp. If we were to go back 100 million years in time we would see a tropical forest here. The weather changes or the tree is just old and dies. The tree falls. In some cases, the trees are covered with mud before they have a chance to decay. If so, then the tree retains its shape under the mud. The tree cells have perished from within. If the cells perish than water fills the spaces where the original cells were.

The water that replaces the cells, is rich in calcium and minerals, such as silicon. If, over time, the water evaporates, the minerals remain in the padded cell old tree, the tree cells are now replaced by minerals. The tree is now petrified but actually it is a blueprint of what it used to be.' John tapped with a special hammer on stones and at the end of the day he had a reasonable collection of fossils. When we walked back, I tripped over a stone. The stone flew off and normally I would not have looked twice. However, if you have been looking at stones for a few hours, you start to see differences between normal and extraordinary stones. It was not a stone!

Now, it was, but it had not always been a stone! I picked it up, it was about the size of a large man's fist. It had a jaw jutting out, in stone. Strong jaw muscles. It looked the most like the head of a giant serpent. Above the jaw muscles was the orbit in which was a petrif ed eye. All one and the same color. There was a line mouth and nose area where you could see the stony structure of the skin It was half a head. The other side showed a cavity where the oral cavity had been and were above the brain cavity with a petrifi ed structure drawing of what had been the brains. 'That' said, John emphatically, 'is a very beautiful fossil. Now, 48 years later it is still on my bookshelf. 'I have always kept it and when I see it, I think back with pleasure to those special two days.

That night we were back in the same rituals, Romney Shed and life repeated itself. Games were played, some folk read and people were bent over a coke talking to each other. I looked at everything with new eyes, I realized that we were here, what used to be 100 million years ago, a primordial sea with dinosaur-like monsters that swam about, long before even one drop of oil was formed.

Extraterrestrial glass

We had just filled our plates for the second time, when the door of the Romney shed flew open and two men came in dark tanned and burnt. 'Hey you,' shouted one of them from afar. 'Tidwell, you old stone knocker'. John turned around and began to chuckle, 'so you sit here eating quietly and in come ground digging scum,' John replied. He left his plate and a moment later the three men were beating each other exuberantly on the back and shoulders. 'What is the food like', asked one of the diggin' scum boys, named Bill? 'The steak was okay', said Tidwell, the stone knocker,' but yes, they fly them in from Texas, they can not mess that up here'. 'Unbelievable, I thought, 'is there anything that doesn't come out from Texas.' 'Geologists and former classmates, of John's ',my father said to me and slightly later he was hailed as exuberantly with,' Golle Gee Big Dan, I thought you were in Saudi.' The oil world is small and us knows us. 'This', said John, 'is my young assistant Daniel, he is big Dan's son' and he pushed me forward. 'Hi there young Dan, 'said the men don't let that old stoneknocker drive you mad.' They were colleagues, but everyone was kind of a professional friend.

There we were a little later with chunks of meat that barely fit on our plate, Yes boy, everything is big in Texas. 'Where have you boys come from now,' Mr. Tidwell wanted to know. 'We landed today, I have come from the *Waw Namus* concessions. Direction Tibest imountains, said Bill, 'and steakboy here and pointed to the second man.,'has been beyond our concessions in Benghazi, towards the Egyptian border, north of *Gilf Kebir*.' I had been among growns-ups for two days without being frowned upon and I asked Bill, 'what did you do there?' 'Well, young Dan', he replied, 'we must ensure that oil continues to come, we are all very important here' and they all laughed.

'Big Dan and his boys must make sure that the stuff comes out of the ground and the right equipment is there to do so and we must make sure that Big Dan knows where that stuff is. Without Big Dan, we can go home and without us, the oil boys can go home, we all need each other badly needed here.' 'That, apart from people like Tidwell who only pick up stones and taps them a bit". And,' I asked, 'is there still oil out there?' 'Oh yes,' said Bill,' always!' 'I,' said the man who was addressed as steakboy, but whose actual name was Dave,' I went to Gilf Kebir with some men to do seismological measurements. The heat was tremendous and the jewels dazzled you if you were not careful.' 'The jewels, do you mean that!' I could not believe what I had just heard. 'Yes', the man said, 'quite disturbing, you should always take care with your tires, driving over them.

'My mouth fell open. 'Doesn't Tidwell teach you anything,' laughed Dave? I have not come there yet,' said John, 'but young Daniel has learned a lot today'. 'Want to hear about it,' asked Dave? 'Boy do I ever,' I said. 'Before we start concessions or lease them, we want to know if it is worth it. So we investigate an area. A natural extension to our company lies beyond Benghazi to Egypt. In our case, an area called Gilf Kebir.' 'Big Dan goes with the technicians to enrich Benghazi with transhipment facilities for supertankers and a refinery'. Moreover, I know now,' filled my father in, that we have the green light for a floating oil line going out at sea to fill supertankers straight from the refinery.' 'Wow,' Dave said, 'big bucks boy, that's gonna cost!'

'That makes Benghazi then, our second major foothold in Libya, so it makes sense that we are going to explore beyond Benghazi.' Bill said, 'yes and I do the same but a few hours away in the other direction at the Waw Namus' 'What is the Waw Namus,' I asked, it began to stagger me. 'A volcano', said Bill as if that was common knowledge. 'Holy cow,' I learned more in two days over Libya than in a few school years.

'But those jewels,' I started again, because I wanted to know. Dave laughed,' they are silicon compounds which occur under high temperature.' 'The ancient Egyptians already picked them up and used them as jewelry'. 'Oh' I asked? 'Oh Yes', the pharaoh Toetankhamon had several incorporated in his amulets'. 'It was not just a dinky old jewel, old Toetank was a very powerful pharaoh and only the best was good enough for him. 'We call it disrespectfully, Desert glass, but in reality, the location is the part of the desert that we call *the large Erg*, the only region in the world where the dunes have been glazed under extremely high temperature and formed 98% pure sio^2. The Egyptians called it the God's stone. it used to be, of course, a hard to reach area, but now with helicopters, ratmobiles and so forth, you're there pretty fast. There are a lot of these jewels being found in caves from the stone age era, where the cavemen, we're talking about 10 000 years ago, made jewelry or cutting objects from this desert glass.'

'Clayton a well known British expedition leader, who in 1932 went looking for the legendary *oasis of Zerzura*, crossed the desert and drove his vehicle as first westerner on to the sea of glass. His tires shattered the plain of jewelry and his car came to a stand still.' Cannot believe it,' I cried out, 'a sea of jewels, I knew nothing about that.' 'There are, I think few people who know this', Dave said. 'You are now one of them' 'Clayton had a document from 1846 in his possession and was looking for a legendary oasis and treasures.''Yep siree, there's been some commotion about the amulet of Toetank', Dave continued. 'The jewel is older than any known Egyptian civilization, therefore, it is millions of years old'. That brought immediately alien theories.' 'What do you think, Dave,' I asked, leaning forward?' Look since antiquity it has been called the God's stone and names always have an origin, but to me that is not a proof.' 'I think that its an old stone, older than the whole amulet, older than any civilization whatsoever, someone fitted it in the amulet, just because someone found it pretty enough, worthy of a pharaoh.'

'I am not into alien conspiracy theories, I just do not believe in them', continued Dave, who now spoke very seriously. 'The problem is that such a vitrification occurs only under extremely high temperatures, such as a nuclear explosion, and I find that difficult to accept as well.' 'Tests to date indicate a fusion of 29 million years ago. If I were to give an explanation, I would tend to speak about the impact of a comet in ancient times. The annoying issue however is that the dunes that are glazed, are not older than 1 million years old. The area covers 6000^2 kilometers. Than you'd expect somewhere a mega crater of the impact.' 'So,' I asked, 'what do you think happened?" I do not know,' Dave said, 'some things just cannot be explained.'

'I can't beat this story', Bill said, 'my volcano area is interesting, but will probably be useless, too much sulphur in the crude oil and then you'd need a process to remove that, but I'm going to pick up a desert.' 'However, we do have answers,' said John Tidwell, pointing to both of us,' young Daniel has today established what the environment here looked like 29 million years ago. '29 million years again,' muttered Dave and we all got up to get an ice cream.

The crotch scratchers

My parents drove off the yard to American friends and we had the place to ourselves. There was not much to do outside than reading in the hot summer, in an environment where every few seconds you'd wave a fly away, you could not do anything. There was nothing to do. I was actually done reading and bored. The Arabic friends were probably playing somewhere else and it would have been too hot to play Doebie, anyway. It was a lazy day. There was always a lot of competition between my brother and me, he was 4 years older than I was, but I was catching up quickly in strength to him. He was still bigger and heavier, very true, but I ran faster and enjoyed to win the games he invented. It must have been frustrating for him to always feel the breath of his younger brother in his neck. My sisters had left with my parents and we just did not want to sit a few hours with their friends. We were king of the castle, when the car disappeared from view.

'What shall we do,' I asked him, as I was drawing on the ground with half a pair of scissors, I had found. 'Start by getting me a coke,' he said. I myself had a craving for a coke as well, so I did not mind. The kitchen was just a few steps from the stairs where we were reading. It bothered me that he wanted to play boss, but I immediately went inside and got two cans of coke. Muhammad came with his donkey cart into the area and drove the cart close to the open garbage drums, empty oil barrels that were filled with household dirt, which was thrown in by the neighbors. He emptied the drums with great regularity and that was fine, because a blind man could find the vessels on scent. In hot countries scents carry, they float, as it were to meet you. 'Please note', my brother said, he's a 'crotch scratcher'. 'A what', I asked? A 'crotch scratcher,' repeated my brother with a bored tone in his voice and took a sip of Coke.

Mohammed shook one of the two barrels and a black cloud of flies fl ew shattered up in the air. He pulled himself together, prepared himself mentally to lift the barrel on to the cart, but then stopped and grabbed his crotch. He clawed and scratched a moment, then pulled the barrel on the cart. 'Didn't I say so,' continued my brother, 'they are all crotch scratchers.' I realized that I had seen scratching Arab men indeed, regularly but it's like with f ies, if you have flies every day around your head, you do not see them anymore and it is more that you feel them than see them before you squat them. A quick movement of the hand to your mouth while you just go on talking or reading.

Is there a day that goes by without you seeing them walking and scratching around,' he went on, his authority in the affirmative, because he had noticed something that had escaped my attention? I did not answer right away, that was another big difference between my brother and me. I took questions seriously and tested it to reality. I let the week outside of our house pass in review. Every day was a bit exaggerated, because my brother was not right there, but in the five days that the school bus was driving through town, I often had seen scratching.

Just when I thought that it might be that one day I might not have noticed the crotch groping, perhaps because I had not been paying attention or I'd been looking at something different, or that if you took an average of more scratching Arabs in ratio to the number of school days, which is a fairly high weekly average spread on display,... I got a thump on my shoulder. 'Are you not listening,' he asked, 'I wanted to know something'. I was always contemplative by nature, a reason why my future wife would tease me and give me the nickname "Pete statistics". I love equation and charts to this day. The thump had been painful and crippled the upper part of my arm and was not distributed because I had not responded quickly enough, but because my brother used it as a reason to give me a thump. He had those annoying power games. He just wanted to manifest that he was the strongest, it must have been uncertainty. He saw the advantage in strength he had, decreasing daily, compared to my age. He also knew that I despised his choice of reading material. Not that I openly said so, but there comes a time when you leave *gunslinger books* or *lord Raffles*, the gentleman thief, far behind you. That time had not yet come for him.

'Yes', I said, 'Arabs scratch their crotch, maybe not the whole day but with great regularity.' 'Arabs, he mimicked after me, scratch their crotch .. This would be a tedious afternoon, and I resolved to not pick a fight.' More to come,' he said, 'not only are they crotch scratchers,' my brother went on in his conspiracy tone of voice, 'but they stink from their fly'.'Holy shit', I thought, 'had been I found or something?' Had I been left and was I adopted later by my parents? It was that I had seen pictures of my father's past and that there was a strong resemblance between us otherwise I might seriously have had my doubts. 'Well,' my brother said as he punched me again on the same spot which had just stopped hurting.

'What do you think.' 'I warn you,' I said, 'do not touch me anymore, because otherwise you'd wish you were far away.' *Crotch scratching Arab far from here*,' mimicked my brother after me, it was clear he was bored rotten and sought a victim.

Never had I found any sign of empathy with either my father or my brother for their fellow man. I was just thinking that it might be a lack of water that Arab people could not wash themselves properly, when I got a shove that almost threw me down the stairs. 'What did I say to you,' my brother wanted to know. Power Games, I realized I had had enough. 'You said Arabs stink from their fly and I find that very interesting.' He looked at me suspiciously not understanding. 'Because', he ..? said, Take it from there sunny boy because ..' Because', I began,' Arabs have no f ies, they have long tent like dresses and if they would have had f ies how close were you to take a good sniff'. I had gone too far, I had pushed my Arab snorting brother over the edge.

He jumped up and said, 'get up now and I'll shut your bloody mouth.' 'No,' I replied quietly, but he did not come closer. I realized that if I got up, he would come up to me and belt me one. If my parents would come home and see one of us with a blue eye, there would be problems. Especially when my brother would say, that I had claimed that he was someone who sniffed Arabic crotches. 'Stand up chicken boy,' he said, 'I am not a coward,' I said, 'leave me alone.' 'Chicken, chicken' started my brother now, how was it possible that this was my brother. 'I warn you,' I said, pointing at him with my half scissor underlining my words. 'Give me those scissors and prove to me that you're not a chicken,' my brother said. I threw the scissors at his feet.

'We're going to do the chicken test,' said my brother, he had probably read it again in some Indian book. I was a bit curious. 'Shoes out,' he said, and kicked his already out. There we were facing each other with bare feet. 'You plant your feet wide apart and taking turns you throw the knife, in this case the scissors, between the feet of the challenger. If the scissors do not stand up in the sand,' my brother pointed out, then you have lost, so you have to throw hard, because the ground is hard,' this was my brother again, the creator of games. Where the scissors remain, you place the right foot and you will not move the left foot. If you pull one of your feet away then you are a coward, the chicken. Is that clear', he asked. It was completely clear to me. Once a trial throw, he dictated. I spread my feet apart and my brother planted the scissors with strength in the ground between my feet.

I realized that those who first threw had the advantage, and I also realized that you had to try to reduce the maximum distance in the middle of the two feet, 'Heads or Tails,' I asked my brother, while I took a piaster coin from my pocket. 'Tails', he said and I flipped the coin up, it came down heads. I tried to put my feet as wide as possible and I waved the scissors half frightfully above my head, and with much force I planted it between the feet of my brother. He moved his right foot and placed it against the scissors half, before pulling it out.

My brother made strange noises and waved the scissors half, from left to right in criss cross movements. Intimidation, I realized, looking past him. He also planted them half down the middle, between my feet. I moved my foot against the handle and pulled the scissors half from the ground. 'I hope I'm not going to throw it in your toe,' I told him. 'Whoa,' my brother said, and raised his hand, 'we agree that no one will speak from now on'. I started to swing, the rusty half in a big circle in again, and let it go. Tooink, the scissors drilled into the ground, 10 inches from my brother's foot. I have to give him credit, he did not pull his foot away.

My brother threw with great force the scissors right between my feet and I thought, what are we doing? But if I stopped now, I would be the chicken and I did not want to grant him that pleasure, probably my brother had the same idea, but we were now on a journey of no return. I grabbed the scissors and how I managed to miss, I do not know, maybe I let go of the scissors too early but it had cut into my brother's foot and I had not been aiming to do so. My brother looked in disbelief at his foot. He lifted it up and immediately groaned in pain. I must have hit a muscle, I thought. I saw a small metal tip sticking out from the bottom of his foot.' Help me, please', he said, and the sweat was beading on his forehead. Good luck, thought the statistician in me, no blood! That came a little later and how. He leaned on me not to place any weight on his foot and we arrived back at the stairs.

He nursed his foot while sitting on the floor by his leg, bent clasping it.' Pull it out,' he said! 'Please,' I said, or 'pretty please.' 'Please, pull it out, God damnit', my brother roared, 'pull it out moron'. It was serious, and I realized I could not let him down. I grabbed his foot with my left hand and he began to moan immediately.' Pull it in one go', he ordered. With my right hand I grabbed the eye of the scissors half and pulled it out, it seemed that it still just snagged on something and when I held it bloodied and already in my hand. It was not so much a wide wound, but a lot of blood came out. My brother pressed hard on the wound and stayed that way for a while. We had both read the same cowboy books. 'Will I burn it shut,' I asked, 'then I'll just get the lighter inside?' Don´t you f... talk stupid,' my brother answered me. After a while the bleeding staunched but my brother kept pain. We put our shoes back on. I was the slave, I prepared sandwiches, made tea and wondered how it would all end. The car came around the corner driving into the yard and my brother and I were reading. Fraternally together. My parents went inside and my sisters set the table. It was a pleasant meal, my parents were in a good mood and many stories were told. My brother was a little quiet but no one noticed.

It was bedtime, and while I was doing the dishes with my sisters, my brother went into the bedroom to study. In time it was bedtime and I remember how I thought, that we had come away well, before I fell asleep. It was weekend and the morning dawned. My brother called me from the other bed.' Can you get some water for me, 'he asked? 'Can you not do that yourself,' I replied. 'I have a terrible pain,' he said, and I got water for him. When we walked to the breakfast table he dragged with his foot. 'What is the matter with you,' asked me mother? 'Oh I've had something in my foot,' he said, 'but it will pass.' Okay this was proof, my brother was not a chicken.

'Let's see,' my mother said, and when she saw his foot she went right panicky and so did I. It was red and swollen. ' Dan,' she shouted to my father, 'come quickly.' My father looked and said, 'oh, that is bad' and he pointed to the red stripe that ran upwards towards the knee. He looked at the foot properly and said, 'you have not stepped into anything, you got something in your foot from the top'. He put his hand on his head and said 'you run a fever.' How has this happened,' he asked in an angry voice?. 'I got a pair of scissors in my foot,' my brother said.' Through and through,' my father wanted to know? How did that happen,' my father asked, and there broke the bubble, my brother looked at me, like he wanted to say,' I can't help it, he really wants to know and said, 'Daniel has thrown it into my foot.' My father looked sharply at me and told my mother, 'your son is mentally ill.' 'He' and my father pointed to my brother,' has got blood poisoning and goes right now with me to the hospital and we'll talk about the scissor stuff later.'

My brother went to the Mossad hospital in Tripoli and had to stay there for some time and our weekend was severely ruined.

The last Barbeque

It was Sunday and we were ready to go to church. That was a privilege because not everyone could go to church in Libya . The only church where a service could be attended was the Lutheran church on the Wheelus air force base. Tripoli had the necessary mosques, where every few hours, a call to prayer was let out. *Allah is God, there is no God but Allah and Mohammed is his prophet.* You did not escape the call, it entered into the smallest corner of Tripoli. With your windows closed the prayer muted somewhat but they would still sneak inside. What had been formerly an imam calling from the minarets, had now been replaced by a loudspeaker system, and I assume that some sort of apprentice priestling now, clicked the play button to start a tape recorder. ***Allah iee Allaaaaaaah***! the words were stretched and held on long. Such a call lasted minutes. Day and night, seven days a week. Where churches in Western countries, chime their bells on Sunday, which is also a call to attend a service, the call in Libya was repeated every few hours.

If you live near a train track, then after a while you do not hear the ringing of the warning bells at a railroad crossing, and if you lived in Tripoli, the Western mind filtered the annoying wailing away. I suppose If they had skipped a call only once, the human mind would have noticed, there is an unconscious recording of events.

It was inconceivable that in a country where people lie down every few hours facing Mecca, someone would start a church or would like to start one. You would be killed if you had such an idea in your head. The same was true for those who wanted to serve a God other than Allah, by renting a room and praying together or singing. No other God should be served but Allah on pain of death. You would be dragged out of that space and be slaughtered like an animal. Your throat would be cut open as with ritual slaughter and you would bleed to death. The same would happen to you if you would insult the prophet Muhammad. If you could escape, an *fatwa* would be spoken over you. This would oblige any Muslim to kill you.

So many years later than the time of our stay in Libya, in 1989 to be exact, a fatwa was spoken out over a British author, Rushdie, by an influential imam in Iran, the Ayatollah Khomeini. The fatwa is a call to kill where ever the infidel is located and in whatever way. The reason was, that part of his book dealt with temptation and the Prophet Muhammad and one of his wives. That was reason enough to condemn a writer to death. Rushdie has been protected since that time and has had no life of his own anymore, because a Muslim may be looming with a knife to cut his throat open. That was only because the Imam took umbrage with the way Muhammad and his family were described.

Let alone that you would offend Allah or dedicate honorary services to a God other than Allah In those 53 years that have passed since the early 60s, there appears to have been no change in the extremist Islamic thought.

An American engineer who held prayer service with some colleagues and their families, for world peace, in my father's office, was fi red and flown back to the States, when his Arab driver caught on to it. The company immediately issued a directive that they would not support staff insulting Islam, in the future, and they prohibited meetings in their buildings other than business. It is not for nothing that the Libyans spoke in a destructive way about every white or any non-Muslim. We were the Christian dogs. The pigs.

You can not be defined worse than being a pig or a dog in a country where these animals are unclean. Those animals you may simply finish off. The tolerance was hard to find. As in India, where every 20 minutes a woman is raped or def led, because men have a different mentality, a mentality that permits that, they found it in Tripoli natural to hate us. It radiated from the houses, and it reflected from the buildings, you felt it float through the streets as an invisible hand that wanted to squeeze you to a pulp and it was present throughout.

If we were hated, the contempt and hatred was even greater for women who were Christian dogs, our wives and our sisters and daughters were in danger, always! There was only one place where they could be stored safely, in their homes. Libyans treated their women as though they were inferior beings, supported or even encouraged by their mosques in this. Imagine our women if they'd go walking about outside without a chaperone or without being covered, well *then it was clear,* they were the whores and hookers and you could offend them.

My mother always looked forward to the Sundays, I assume she was a believer in a pure way that needed no church, but she enjoyed those few hours Wheelus airbase, and so did the other Western ladies, the church service and then gather together, with coffee and donuts and they saw it as an escape from the 'hatred world' that surrounded them daily. Americans from oil companies were always welcome with a pass on the base and we had a pass to worship on Sundays.

At Wheelus airbase the military attended with their families the service and they did not notice as much as us the outside world. It was a bit of moved America, a village plucked from the States and put down behind a fence with military posts. In addition to the officers mess, a room which they had renamed Chapel. It was a place where a Lutheran worship service was held every Sunday. Oh well, every denomination was welcome, and Luther would have wet his eyes as the Catholics, whom he had fought as a Protestant sat fraternally together with the Lutherans, sharing the folding chairs.

The pastor was Captain Mackletan, a fighter pilot, who had felt the call by absence of a minister or pastor to observe the congregation. He was a jovial man who loved socializing. He greeted everyone with a handshake at the entrance of the hall. The Lutheran service under Captain Mackletan was very short. The captain was short of text, he did a reading and he did not sing. So no old American ladies choirs or psalms, just a prayer, a reading and then coffee and donuts. Sometimes, he would say, under the coffee, 'have I given the blessing now or haven´t I?' That was meant seriously and often we knew it no longer. Then he asked if everyone would stop for a moment and then he blessed us again, 'it never hurts, an extra blessing', he said. A pragmatic man in a strange setting.

As jetfighter trained to destroy and kill, and on the Sunday talking about love and peace. There were a few soldiers who attended the service, among them was a lieutenant, named Steven, and slowly but surely he became infatuated with my sister. My sister was a beauty, a real classic beauty. Steven had a friend named Kermit, a name which was then not yet associated with green plush animals and at times, when my father was home, they came along with a jeep from the base and had dinner with us. They were single boys who were innocently young and had been sent to Tripoli. They were out there, and it was obvious they missed family life and a meal with others, they were military colleagues. Steven came from Nebraska and Kermit from Minesota.

It was just nice to not hear a heavy Texan accent. My sister blossomed up when she saw Steven and Kermit had told me that Steven was very shy but wanted ask my sister to be his fiancé when his tour of duty in Libya expired. That would be in a few months. He had bought a ring and Kermit had helped him sort one out and Kermit said that he always carried it in his pocket over his heart. I believed it, I had seen that when my sister went to the kitchen, the two friends looked at each other and more than once Steven then touched secretly his buttoned shirt pocket.

The service was shorter than normal, and Captain Mackletan did a reading on the Last Supper. 'It's not Easter,' he said, and we are far from it in time, but I think it is an appropriate and beautiful reading. The prayer was not the standard prayer, but a prayer so from his heart, emotional, one of the most beautiful prayers I've ever heard. Everyone felt that there was something extraordinary in progress. Patches I remember and I will never forget. It was not the unctuous liturgy, but a cry of despair filled with melancholy. '*Lord, dear Lord*', he said, '*we are here to worship you, we are your people. Bless my enemies so they will treat your people with grace Bless us all, in the times to come, I love you, my Lord, in Jesus name thank you for everything*', everyone said amen and thus ended a remarkable prayer.

We looked a little strange around us, the atmosphere had become very serious.' Can I have your attention just a bit longer,' have said the captain. I have ordered a barbeque, I know that we actually have a barbeque every second week, but I always find it so cozy and I have my reasons. I can no longer be your pastor and I have to follow my duty. I didn't see it coming, I did not totally understand what was happening. It has pleased the base commander to give some of us a promotion spoke our old predecessor. From tomorrow on, I'll be Major Mackletan and flight lieutenant Steven was promoted to eskaderon flight leader and Captain. My sister looked very proud. Lieutenant Mckeely is from tomorrow on Captain Mckeely. I would suggest that Lieutenant Kermit perceives the pastor's role, he is not promoted, I want to congratulate him. We have been told last night that we had been promoted, and tomorrow we leave for our next destination. My sister looked bewildered, Steven looked unhappy at the ground, with a red head. 'Father, where are you going,' my mother asked? '**Nam**' 'has knocked at our door, for us', said Major Mackletan, '**Vietnam**.' The barbeque went joyless, when everyone had spoken and shaken hands, I said to Kermit, 'it's not nice for my sister but it's good that Steven was promoted captain, right.' Kermit looked at me and said, 'you're a good boy, but you do not know the world.' 'Why,' I asked? 'They are not just sent to Nam, they are sent to a bad place in Nam. It is customary on the basis that you are promoted then, the widow's pension is higher.The scales fell from my eyes, the reading about the last supper, the remarkable prayer that suddenly became crystal clear to me. Congratulations to Kermit because he was not promoted.

Steven said, 'I gotta go, I have to pack and I do not feel well'. He walked over to my sister and looked at her long and said,'I have loved you most of all in my life, I'll write you. He saluted to show esteem. My sister just nodded, speechless. I stood next to her and I could look in Steven's heart and what I saw was despair and a love that was really pure. He clicked his shoes together, turned and marched with away with stiff passes, not looking back. Never looking back.

'God willing, we will be here talking in about six months, said the new major and he said, 'I want to repeat what Jesus said,' 'let the children come to me.' When I hesitated, he said, 'you too boy'. He had a word for each of us. To a girl, he said,' you always had those beautiful curls, which I will never forget,' and he kissed her. It struck me that he spoke in the past tense. To a boy, he said,' I am so proud of you, you were a joy in your home.' Each child was briefly exposed. To me he said, 'you 'll be a good man later, I can see that'. 'Good luck father,' I said. '*There lies no glory in killing*,' he said, and he looked at me and said '*remember me*' and I have done so and I am not ashamed of the tears from my eyes while I am writing this.

Before he walked away he again assured us that God willing, we would come together again in six months . God was not willing, and he opened the door to ugly Nam, the doorway through which his people were sucked in and closed it behind them, leading them into ruthless hatred, and made them crash in clusters of fireballs.

The first letters were positive in nature and Steven wrote what he had never dared to ask. He counted the months and days, and then he wanted to talk with my parents and my sister, serious talk about how he wanted to give his life, contents. After a few months the first bad news came, captain Mckeely was killed. Steven wrote about the number of missions that were flown. The number was greatly increased, from a few per week to daily missions. The fatigue of his colleagues and how fed up he got. On the other hand, said our optimistic friend, the time passed quickly and he wanted to know if my sister wanted to marry a farmer because, as his months were almost over, he never wanted anything to do more with the Air Force. He wanted to grow crops with his father and brother in Nebraska.

God was not willing to Major Mackletan, he would never share a barbeque with us again, he went down burning. Steven now wrote bitter letters, a lot of soldiers died. They were not fighting against Vietnam, they fought against Russian advisors and their weapons, he was tired, but he only had six weeks to fly and then he'd come back, first he would go past his parents in Nebraska and then come to Tripoli.

It was in the afternoon and I was alone with my sister at home when a jeep stopped from the airbase. Kermit came walking out and he had a letter in his hand, he looked pale. We sat down at the table. It is not Steven, asked my sister? Kermit said, I'm here to honor my friend. This is a letter addressed to me, said Steven ..He read it with a screwed voice, *Kermit, buddy when you read this letter, we will not meet in this life anymore. I'm tired, worn down, the only thing that still keeps me going is the counting of days on the calendar, as a promise of a better life. Just three weeks after the mission tonight. I worry a lot we have been flying more missions, there is hardly time for maintenance on the machines. I dreamed last night about Major Mackletan he wanted to talk to me. I put this letter on my desk addressed to you, enclosed the ring for my beloved, I will do this every mission, if you receive this letter, put the ring in her hands.* Kermit took a ring out of the envelope and the three of us started crying our eyes out.

Jane

The school bus turned on to the parking field and came to a halt in a cloud of dust. The Italian Matrone, who has watched over us began pushing against children, and within seconds we were outside. The stream of children now began to seek their way from the various buses to the main entrance. I followed the f ow with my satchel and Donald Duck lunch box, sometimes simple things change and sometimes they don't. Dust whirled up where we walked. Soon our boots were colored gray. I made my way through the gate and we were in the complex, an American junior high school, plucked from America and planted in the desert, with a student population of Texas. A cloud of dust came racing down the field and an old convertible Cadillac stopped with dust settling around it. The boy that got out the car did not open the car door but simply jumped out. He leaned in over the back door with turned down windows and picked up some books from the back seat. He was what my classmates would call cool.

He had no crew cut, where each boy at that time had millimetered hair. He just picked up a little boy by the arm and said, carry my books, and he pushed them into his arms and walked whistling behind us through the gate. He did not have to make his way through the crowd. The crowd dispersed where he walked. he was cool he radiated stoneage primacy . This was someone without restraint. We had just witnessed the arrival of Jimmy Hurt. He did not have to push and squeeze, he simply walked as if there was no one around him. How was it possible that you could come to school in your own car? 'He has no license,' told my friend Keith, who walked beside me. 'He just crabs his mother's car, and does what he feels like.' 'How do you know', I asked?' He came to live in our neighbourhood', replied Keith. Well American cars were easier to drive than my brother's beetle. Our American neighbor had an American car, but like most of those big tanks, they almost without exception, they were automatics. You kept your foot on the pedal and you put the gear stick in D from drive, and you drove away when you released the brake, a bit like bumper cars at the fair.

'His mother can't go on the street with the Arabs here,' said Keith 'and his father works in the desert, and the car is there anyway.' We crammed our books and gym outfits in our locker and we went to the f rst lesson. It was Monday, and so after a signal through the intercom, everyone got up and vowed a pledge to the flag. With your right hand on your heart and your eyes blurred with a faraway look, you began to recite: **I pledge allegiance to the flag of the United States of America and to the republic for All which it stands, one nation under God indivisible, with liberty and justice for all.** Later I realized how clear these rituals are, it takes only a few seconds to complete, but the words hone in to the point where you think you have invented them yourself. You support the republic, you do not allow, because of the word indivisible, that a state would want to separate itself and you put yourself under one God. That's clever marketing. Where ever immigrants come from, after a few years of reciting these texts would feel connected to the flag and support America. It breeds a sense of unity. Are you ready the master began, now for the school anthem and he set in. **we are proud to share thy honor, proud to bear thy name and we stand in awe and reference praise thee, oh O.C.S. In the midst of the sandy desert besides the shining sea stands a school that fills our hearts with pleasant memories, we are proud to bear thy honor and proud to bear thy name.**

This was also a gem of marketing. Later in your life you would, by the frequent singing of our school song, really believe in the pleasant memories and the pride of the name of the school. In reality, my first year had not been so very been pleasant. The bullies from Texas had kicked me under my ass as I had walked with my books under my arm, I had been beaten, bullied, teased and harassed: **stands, a school that fills our hearts with pleasant memories.** The passing of the years makes up for it and now when I look back, I believe they were pleasant years. Only when I became part of the Texan cock order did my pleasant memories begin. I wonder whether the pleasant memories of the school bullies are the same, looking back with joy of mistreating fellow students, or has a layer of false sentiment been pasted over us all by the passing of time. A layer that has been deposited in a way that we really believe that we had friends, a great school, and above all, that we were diligent and obedient.

Indoctrination does things to you, it gives you a false past. A false togetherness that never existed. The only truth abiding in the school song was the location, **in the desert, next to the sea.** I also understand now that you could not **sing Kicked off the bus by a common fat bitch, stumbling with boots against the scorpions and other vermin, paving your way, coughing in the dust strained by desert sand, and running in circles around fi elds with 40 ° C with a taste of blood in your mouth... Oh O.C.S!**

Although such a text would have been more truthful, they would have evoked the unpleasant images. Images that show a life of children who were placed for a few hours a day in a surrounding where they had to fend for themselves at the mercy of all sorts of nasty outside influences, over which they had no control. The door opened and the vice principal came in, 'I want to present a fine young man, your new friend and classmate'. 'Welcome, Jim,' said our teacher, I was expecting you, you are on my list, I think you're going to have a right nice time here. That's Jim Hurt, sir, and I do as my name says. Hurt, I understood it, he could hurt people, Jimmy Pain, he could hurt people and he looked it as well.

Now he would get scolded, I thought, because you never had the last word in our school, and you treated teachers with respect. 'So Hurt', said Mr. Harper,' from now on, *you speak when spoken to*'. 'You talked to me, sir, and I must convey the greetings of my father who is with the school board'. 'Find somewhere to sit, Hurt,' said Mr. Harper with a gracious smile.' Have a good day,' said the vice principal and disappeared from our lives. 'What are you doing Hurt', Mr. Harper asked when Hurt moved through the classroom from right to left and then remained standing. 'My name is Jimmy, sir, you said so yourself.'

'I want a place where I can see and hear you properly'. We all realized what was happening, Jimmy Hurt was an expert in baiting and sucking but in a way that he was always covered. I'll see you here after school', Mr. Harper said, wanting to start the lesson and did not feel like a Monday morning power struggle. 'That will not do, sir', he said, 'with all due respect, I have to bring my car down the garage for a tune up'. We were all 13 and 14 years old. Keith and I looked at each other, grinning, and the girls looked with admiration at the new man who had entered the classroom. 'Get up', said Jimmy to a boy, 'you're in my seat.' Grab all your books, said Mr. Harper and thereby lost the unequal power struggle with Jimmy Hurt, whose father was on the board and therefore the employer of Mr. Harper and probably a hotshot in the oil company.

Mr. Harper drew some triangles on the black board and in the meantime talked about equal angles, when Jimmy Raised his hand and simply began to speak. 'Mr. Harper, sir, if you speak will you please turn around? You sound really unclear and and you lisp,' I cannot follow you.' No one laughed, it was mean, Mr. Harper lisped indeed, but was a great person and a good teacher who always made time for you. There was a silence. Mr. Harper had turned red. 'James', he said 'what are you doing here? Why are you here?' 'I am 16,' said Jimmy, which explained his size and muscularity, I have to wait another year before I can go to conscription.' We all understood it what he was saying, in your 17th year, you could sign up for the army with consent of your parents.

I hope I can give you, before you are going to serve our country, a nice f nal school year. Shall we agree that it is going to be a pleasant year?' 'Yes sir,' said Jimmy Hurt and that concluded what could have been a right unpleasant year. Wherever we had classes, Jimmy doodled and he just read Gi Joe magazines out loud. He was simply ignored. However, he still intentionally knocked classmates over in passing them and he messed people up. He was a frustrated person who always wanted to confirm his physical superiority. Alas, we left him to himself.

Meanwhile, the year progressed, and a new gymnasium was completed, it was a multi-purpose hall where you could listen to a speech by the principal or could watch indoor sport competitions. It had a wooden f oor with a tangle of lines and lines in various colors which made it suitable for various indoor games, at both sides there were wooden bleachers and... it had air conditioning , which was very modern! The boys could now choose between running and training for the American footbal team, which was hard going in the heat outside, or you could sign up for boxing and that took place in the sports hall. For me the choice was easy, I asked my parents to sign a no liability note which the school required and instead of running in the deadly heat, I trained in the cool gym.

There you had to skip ropes in groups and hit punching bags. They gave you special gloves and we almost felt the equals of Cassius Clay who later would become Muhamed Ali. In reality, it was quite hard work. The instructor blew a whistle and you'd change from skipping rope to hitting the punching bags, alternating it all the time and despite the air conditioning, a predominant sweat odor spread through the gym. After a few weeks of dancing around and jumping ropes to improve our endurance improved, we got to fight. Teeth protectors in, head protection gear on and wrists taped inside your gloves. You switched partner every two minutes when mr Gadjul blew his whistle. Boxing rounds are always 2 minutes, with a 1 minute break. A full boxing match consists of 12 rounds and then you're burned up.

We became incredibly fit, we jumped rope, danced around with fake jabs and then it was boxing time. Mr. Gadjul organized his lessons well, after a while he appointed one of us each lesson, as whistle blower, who would get a stopwatch around his neck and he himself would walk about and observe the fighting pairs.' No', he would shout then and would show us some moves. After a month we were pooled and we were fighting each other. I had an incredible advantage, as it turned out, and that benefi t was due to the length of my arms. I could touch people who could not get to me. The only one with comparable arm length was mister Gadjul. One day he called me aside,' if you really want to score', he said, 'you lean into your blow with your shoulder behind it, in a straight line with your fist and leaning with your toes as pivot point, forward. Then you put the power of your arm and your weight into the blow and the potential is much greater.'

I started practising it, and after a few weeks you'd recognize the feeling and moment. When the opportunity presented itself and I leaned into my blow, then my opponent would go down like a block. 'Break,' mr Gadjul, would cry then and then you had to stop. Sometimes a blow came through your defense and it always struck me that muffled by the glove, it never hurt only a day later when your jaw went stiff or blue. 'Who knows what a window is', Mr. Gadjul asked one day. A window? We looked at him in amazement. 'What do you mean sir,' a boy asked? 'A window is a window'! 'That's very good', said mr Gadjul. 'You can look through a window. In boxing you also have windows. The boxing window. Always seek the window with your strokes. It is the part between the boxing gloves of your opponent which is not protected. The window comes and goes, so you must act quickly when you see it, you have to act when you see it,' we all nodded. Mr. Gadjul had really boxed in his younger year and you could tell.

Meanwhile, Jimmy became a sports legend in school, he could do push-ups most often of all, he ran the fastest. .He threw the disc over the fence. The shotput, no one could cast it as far as he could. Everything that had to do with brutal force, was written on his skin. He was defender in his team and climbed over some other rugby players to get to the attackers. Outside the sporting events he bullied people, he kicked them as they happened to walk where he wanted to walk, he appointed stooges that had to carry his books, and if he felt like it, he simply belted someone. He was primitive.

Nothing would have happened if it had not been for a new girl in our class. She introduced herself with, 'I'm Jane' and Jimmy breathed deeply and said in a loud voice, 'I'm Tarzan and I love pussy'. Jane looked at him and said I could have sworn you were his friend the monkey.' I burst out laughing and with me half the class. Who thought that was funny, asked Jimmy, and he looked around scrutinizing. I do not know why, but I said,' I found that very funny' and expected that I would get support but no one laughed anymore. 'Well', said the teacher,' now that we know that, Jane why don't you find yourself a seat.' Jane went into the front seat next to me. When the bell rang, I smiled at her and asked, 'shall I carry your books?' She gave me a heavenly smile, 'of course, Tarzan, thanks.' 'My real name is Daniel,' I replied, and together we walked out of the classroom where the primate was already waiting.

'Hey,' he began,' isn't that our pussy boy?' A few followers laughed to please him. I wanted to say something clever, and answered, 'you have to be one to recognize one' and walked on with my books under one arm and Jane's under my other arm. I heard a growl behind me and got a push that almost made me fly forward. 'Am I a sissy ,'asked Jim intimidatingly,' a pussy boy?' 'About as big as they come,' I said, and I realized that my words would have terrible consequences for me. 'Ok **Pussy boy,** say that again, in my face', muttered Jim and I saw him tighten his muscles and letting them go and tightening them again.' Why don't I say that to you after school,' I answered, 'tough man that I was", I am walking with a lady'. Women have always had that kind of effect on me. 'After school pussy boy, outside the fence,' Jim growled. 'I hope you won't forget,' I said.

I was very worried, whether I would still be alive be after school. Keith said, 'man you really told him off, hey he had it coming!' 'What do you think Keith,' I asked,' do I stand a chance?' 'No way, replied my friend, 'no possibilities there I am afraid. You do not stand a chance, he will beat you up and kill you and then he'll wipe his boots off your forehead.' His words gave me some horrible images. The morning flew by and before we knew it we were in our homeroom class with our lunch box. Keith was being consulted by many boys and then theatrically would write a name on a list. Jimmy sat back and pointed at me without saying anything, and I knew I was living on borrowed time.'

Are you with me in the pool', Keith asked me?' What pool', I wanted to know? 'Well the betting pool on who is going to win. You put a quarter in or three quarters on the favorite and you pocket three times." I suppose I'm not the favorite,' I said. 'No, not really'. said Keith frankly. 'Who has laid in', I wanted to know? 'The whole class except for Jim and you. I like it so much, man, a fight, nothing ever happens around here'.. 'Has anyone bet on me,' I wanted to know. 'Yes,' said Keith, 'one person'. 'Thank you Keith,' I started ... but he interrupted me. 'Nothing personal but I bet on Jim.' 'Jane has bet on you.' 'Thanks for nothing', I said.

'Hey pussy boy', Jim said," I want to talk to you outside, in private about a few rules that we will abide.' He got up and beckoned me.' I think you're shit' he said 'and if I come across you later in life, I'll kill you, but I only have a few days to go and then I'm 17, I don't want to be suspended and not join the army'. 'So,' I asked? 'It's gone too far', he said, 'neither of us can still walk away from here.' But if we are just outside the gate and make a lot of racket, a teacher is bound to separate us and then we can both walk away with our head up high. I could hardly believe this, the intimidating Jim wanted to make a deal.' Do you hear me dickhead', he asked me? 'Yes, we could do it', I replied. 'Nice,' growled Jim as he walked back into the classroom , and over his shoulder he said, 'okay no knives.' The class froze. The final bell rang and I did not feel at ease, Would Jim really enter into a sham fight or was it trick to immediately kill me off? The large group of boys clung to me and hurried me on as we walked to the gate. Outside the gate a semi-circle was formed. The air was charged, the excitement fluttered over the group back and forth. Jane stood at bay with some girls watching. I wished she had never made that bad joke about monkeys and Tarzan, it shot through me. I gave my books to a boy of our bus and asked if he wanted to keep them. I said out loud,' I don't see **puss'n boots**, anywhere. Maybe he's shitting himself.'

'Are you talking about me, moron,' came a hoarse voice behind me, 'come here, I'll kill you.' He made a great fuss, screaming and cursing. **'I am here chicken boy**,' I cried, 'I smell you but I don't see you'. An angry growl was the answer. Suddenly I knew you could not trust fate. One of us would sooner or later violate the agreement. I realized that I would have to be that one. He came to me with a lot of clamor and gave me a push and wanted to kick me. He missed, the rope jumping had made me fast. I stepped aside and he passed me like a mad bull. Now he was standing with his back to the bus. I pulled my shoulders up and I popped them a bit together. Screaming and cursing he came a step forward and I … I saw the boxing window, the window! I leaned forward on my toes and with all the strength of my right arm, with my weight behind it I hit him just above his nose on his forehead. He brought his left hand up and I hit him now with two short blasts on the side of his head. In the gym people would have fallen over. His head snapped back and he really banged the back of his head into the bus. For a minute his face got a silly expression and then he roared out because of the betrayal. I was saved by the bell .. Boys came running, 'teachers are coming,' they cried. I hurried away and I was followed by a murderous Jim. I sprinted into the bus, the doors closed behind me and the driver drove away. *'Kill you,'* it sounded from outside. I looked through the window and waved friendly to Jim who saw purple. So I made a finger to top it off. My knuckles were skinned and my wrist ached. I had sprained it. I felt sick, school sick the next day and my mother thought that was rather nice.

When I went back to school after the weekend I feared the meeting with Jimmy. The bus stopped and I hopped out and sprinted to our classroom. The children all came in, all except Jimmy. Keith came in and immediately raised his thumb, 'Hi tiger,' he greeted me.' A few days ill?' 'Yes,' I said,' a summer flu or something'. You've missed Jimmy's goodbye party' he said. 'What a pity,' I exclaimed. 'Well with Jimmy on our side, Vietnam can simply forget it.. 'yeah,' said Keith, 'he was quite strong' and I could not believe my luck.

The underwater club

'These are the membership cards,' said my father, holding up some cards, 'don't lose them!' We took the cards and looked them over with great attention, underwater explorer's club , it read in fancy letters.' O ur family has become member of the club', continued my father. 'Where is that club,' we asked 'and what can we do there'? 'It is a restaurant with a swimming pool and a fenced off piece of beach with guards monitoring it.

There are no Mo's. It is located in Giogimpopoli, and the entrance is opposite Guys and Joe's ... there is a country road that leads towards the beach and then you come to the complex.' I had heard at school about Guys and Joe's. It was a real burger bar. Not like McDonalds now, but a kind of kiosk along the road with a baking tray where someone made burgers for you.I had never been there since the schoolbus took me and brought me to my house and drove past it. It came closest to something American that was run by an Arab. It had two partners a man from Texas with an Arab who baked everything and ran everything. In Tripoli, you always needed to have an Arabic partner. Given the name of the kiosk, the investor and owner must have been called Joe. It had been a great success. The type of business that you do not miss if it is not realized, but once present it is impossible to imagine life without it. Guys and Joe's. 'So you turn to right,'my father said, 'otherwise you get to the bowlerina. If you see that, you are too far.'

The bowlerina was a project of an Italian who had started a bowling alley with an Arab partner. It was not a great bowling alley, but it was a place where you and your family could go. Arabs, in their long robes would not go bowling. Neither would their children and wrapped up women The prices they charged would discourage an every non Westerner. Now there was also a diving club! 'The company pays an annual membership,' my father said, 'and that is a good thing because it is ridiculously expensive.'The company bent over backwards to please the workers and technicians. 'Your sisters and your mom can swim there without being pestered.' Unbelievable, I thought. 'Why are there no Arabs,' I asked? 'They can not pay it and it's private club you can only get in with a membership card.' 'Why can't they pay it,' asked my brother? 'Look,' said my father, membership is 250 pounds per year. the only Arabs that can afford it are men of a different class, there's no problem there. But they still have to be accepted by a commission'. That was a barbaric high amount, the owners with their Arab partner had an even better deal than Guys and Joe's or Bowlerina. A pound was in the 60's worth 10 guilders, at a time when a monthly salary in the Netherlands was 300 guilders, the cardboard membership card was worth 2500 guilders. Eight Dutch monthly salaries.

'What are we exploring,'asked my brother, who had visions of scuba dive tanks and deep caves. 'No diving,' replied my father, 'it's just a name we came up with.' 'There is a restaurant with a wall around it and a swimming pool and a bit of beach.' 'The beach is worth nothing, it is rocky and full of seaweed. We can go this Saturday for a swim and then Sunday to Wheelus airbase to church.' My mother was particularly delighted now she had two outings when my father was not in the desert.

We turned right before Guys and Joe's and at the end of a long country road we came to a fence with a guard next to it and a long high bright white wall. My father showed his ticket and the man saluted and opened the gate. First you walked past a restaurant part and what a luxury! Not to be seen anywhere in Tripoli. Tables were laid with linen and napkins neatly folded with cutlery next to it, waiting for the "underwater explorers", to have something to eat, once they were done swimming. That was normal in the Netherlands, but here you just forgot that another world existed outside Libya. This was a piece of European civilization put behind a fence with a guard in front of it, specifically for those who could afford the ticket.

It was not really special to mention except that you could simply walk around unthreatened. My sisters and mother in a bathing suit with a large umbrella over them and my brother and me jumping off the diving board and rushing down a water slide. There were some Texan friends from my school splashing about and it was great fun. For the first time in my life I heard Buddy Holly, with his Peggy Sue and we were again included in the march of civilization, the bad dream full of hate was outside the fence and would not be permitted to enter by the guards.

If you knew, Peggy Sue, Then you know why I feel blue, my
Peggy peggy sue oh oh .. my ..

The melody filled my heart and for the first time in my life I had heard rock 'n' roll and I was hooked, it was found to have been released in 1958 but it had not reached the Libyan coast until the underwater club opened its gates and played it from the soft drink bar in the 60's.I asked if I could see the sleeve and the bartender gave it in my hands, Buddy Holly was the spitting image of my brother! Tall with owl glasses and brylcreme that held his hair flat. Like Buddy Holly, my brother would be killed a few years later, and die a horrible death, but we luckily did not know at the time and the day was carefree and full of happiness. We joined in with some Texan boys and girls, who had just become member, and were of our age and we walked to the beach. What a stinking mess, if you've never smelled what washed up, dying and drying seaweed smells like. You can't imagine it, but take my word for it, it stank.

As my father, had already told us, a rocky beach, such as you encounter in Malta, with piles of smelly seaweed. I walked little ways into the water wading through seaweed, but it was scary to do and suddenly I felt something sharp. A wave had pushed me into rock, first you did not see it but a cut opened up on my leg that was not bleeding but was white, surgical deep, the rocks were razor sharp, you'd be crazy if you went diving there. I understood that the name was indeed conceived and that none of the Underwater explorer's club members would ever have the intention of diving

I was like a war wounded soldier supported and led back to the soda bar where the bartender had a first aid kit. 'Why do you want to swim in the sea,' he asked me, 'with sharks and eels, and sharp rocks. It's more fun here'. If we had not known already, it was now confirmed, this was not an underwater exploration club! He cleaned the wound with boric water and dressed it, saying 'you're lucky, you could have cut a tendon. Janet and Debbie, two Texan girls did not leave my side, they had found an excuse to mother me and waged a real battle to be nominated best nurse. It would be the start of a friendship that would last until the 1967 war, when fate cruelly drifted us apart. 'You know what we are to do tomorrow,' said my father to my brother? ' We'll go and take a look to see if your car has arrived yet'. Than you can go on your own to the club if I work in the desert.

So my brother, my father and I went to town the next day and we arrived at the showroom where my father had done the deposit for my brother's cream-colored beetle, but ... there was something very wrong. The showroom was still there but there were now a couple of desks in it and it looked like a sort of administrative centre. My father asked the owner for the VW dealership. Shoulders were shrugged and we were being stared at as if we were half crazy. There was an English speaking Arab who came up to us and asked if he could help my father.

My father repeated that he came for a VW. 'No, no', said the man, and he smiled politely, 'they have left'. 'What do you mean, left', my father said. 'Away,' the man said, we are a tax office. 'Where have they gone to', asked my father? The clerk shrugged. 'Egypt? He did come from there,' he replied. He did not know. My father knew what to do,' I will put the lawyer of the company on it and then we'll find out', he said. The clerk walked away, indicating that our talk was over and we were left standing in the office. My father had made a down payment of a quarter of the car's value and did not go away, but the new occupants of the room had nothing to do with it.

Ultimately, we all three went away deeply disappointed. My brother because his beetle had disappeared into the money flow of a corrupt Arab. I, because I realized that we could not go so easily to the Underwater Club and my father because he saw his deposit evaporate before his eyes. So it was, that my brother bought a second hand American car from a church member at Wheelus airbase, it was a tank, a Ford Fairlane 500 1958, you could feel the power of the car trembling under your feet and the sound was a deep V8 rumble. **bo bo bo boh ..** It was a mean machine, and in retrospect I think it was a more comfortable car than the beetle would ever have been. The downside was that they really hated you now, because they mistook you for an American. Thus began a summer of many visits to the underwater club.

The dance

As so often we were reading in the garden, my brother had a bunch of "lord Raffles the gentleman thief", right next to him, and once again I reread the National Geographic. My brother's foot had healed well, you did not notice that a scissor had gone half through. He had dragged his foot for a while, but I guessed that he did so to impose a sense of guilt on me and was looking for attention. It was one of those days, warm and languid, filled with fl ies. I had to do some homework but it was Friday afternoon and Monday seemed like an eternity away. There were all these little things that always needed your attention. You should never drink thoughtlessly, even though your book was ever so exciting. You should always check if your glass was free of bugs. You should never drink from a can or you had to always keep your thumb over the opening. Shoes, you never just put on, you always held them upside down. Nine out of ten times you did so in vain, the greater your gratitude if you were rewarded the tenth time by a bug falling out of your shoe.

Such is life in warm regions. That is not bad, you get used to it quickly. It was always wiser to eat citrus fruits instead of sweet fruit, it is not to be imagined what for extras you'd find in sweet fruits. You'd know of course after you'd bitten an insect in half. So we sat there facing my brother's Ford Fairlane, and his car had a radio, but not one like you would have today with presets, but one with thick chrome buttons. Arabic wailing came out of the speakers. I Love Oriental music, but not the elongated bleating that surrounded you all day in Libya. To be fair, it must have been pretty difficult for the singers to elongate the sounds as they did, without breathing in between. There was always a drum to be heard in the background.

The Ford was from 1958 but was well ahead of its time. Power steering and automatic transmission, the power brakes and electric windows that opened and closed at command. The trunk was big enough to transport a few dead bodies if you were a gangster, or if you were differently inclined, more bags and suitcases than you could ever need. The doors just like the beetle's of his classmates, closed with a solid metal sound. Kedonk, the door was closed, and if you'd catch your hand in between, then it would be irrevocably broken. That sort of car. The Ford had a long bench up front where you could easily sit with three, side by side.

It had something extraordinary, it had air conditioning! My father's Opel didn't have that!. The huge power house of an engine was not focused on speed, but in order to make all those subsystems function flawlessly. The odometer went in miles and stopped at 100 miles. At a time when European cars could barely come above 120 kilometers per hour, this monster, flew, low over the road at 160 kilometers per hour. On the other hand, It drove 10 miles on a gallon. Which converted to three and a half kilometers per liter.

Across America, the maximum speed was 70 miles per hour, so it was an overkill of power to just to catch up quickly or to pass another car. For the rest you needed a big engine to move the car. The weight of that Ford must have been enormous. So my brother looked occasionally, with pleasure, at his creme blue monster. I had my own bit of pleasure, next to me, it was a bb gun, which I had saved for. Laying apart my pocket money for many months. Our American neighbor had bought it for me on Wheelus airbase.

The sign on it read: Daisy outdoor products. It had a pump action system, just as the Winchester rifles in the cowboy films. It fi red round brass bullets, the size that you have in a bicycle wheel ball bearing, or that you might find like a shiny decoration on a cake. You brought a piston to readiness moving the barrel back and forth, and then you could shoot. At the top was a loading chamber, a hole the size of the pellet and you could load 20 bullets in one time. You could shoot quite accurately up to 30 meters and then gravity started working against you. It warned you not to shoot at people because the bullets would penetrate the skin, even if you wore jeans. Typical American disclaimers, I thought, of course, you were not going to shoot at people.

You should also wear glasses, continued the disclaimer because the bullets, unlike lead pellets did not flatten by impact, but could bounce and ricochet. I certainly was not going to wear safety glasses, I had made my mind up, because that would make it very difficult to aim. It was fun to put a pencil upright and try, after careful considerations to shoot it in half. I was actually shocked when I hit it one time, the pencil had gone right through the middle. It had something addictive to it, you'd point at something and moments later it was gone. I put the bb gun down between my brother and went back to read.

My father came out with my mom, 'we are going to visit acquaintances', he said, do you want to come along?' We did not feel like going. 'We won't be long, don't do anything stupid', my mother asked, 'scissors and stuff?' 'No,' we said, we had not forgotten.' Well, see you later then,' my parents said, and we waved them out. 'I', said my brother, 'would like a coke and you may get it for me.' I had no problem there because I was going to get drink for myself anyway. 'Okay,' I replied as I walked up the three steps to get to the kitchen.

When I came back with the coke in my hands, my brother was inspecting with great interest my bb gun. 'It lies comfortably in the hand,' he said and he pumped the barrel back and forth. 'Hey,' I said, it is loaded you know, and now you have charged it. 'How many bullets are in there,' in he asked? 'It is full, about twenty shots or so,' I said, and an alarm bell went off in my head. 'That's a lot of shots,' my brother said, 'wait a moment, I think I can shoot the can out of your hand.' Do not act disturbed,' I replied. 'I mean it,' he said, 'do not move'.

I now held the cans behind my back. I saw that he did not like that. 'Do not come closer, my trigger finger is getting nervous,' he continued. 'Shit my brother was reading too many of those crappy cowboy stories.'

I was back at square one, I was not adopted, I knew, because I looked like my father in appearance, they probably found him, my brother, somewhere in a shoebox. I made quick decisions, if I would defy him by saying, 'you won't shoot,' he would surely shoot, I was suddenly convinced of that, because he would see that as a challenge that he could relate to. I decided to keep my mouth shut. 'We still have to finish a conversation,' my brother said.' Arabs scratch their crotches'. They are crotch scratchers'. 'No, hey,' I thought,' not again' 'yes,' I said in a neutral tone. 'They stink from their fly,' he continued. 'Oh,' I answered and I realized how threatening it is when a gun is pointed at you. 'Don't you think that they stink from their fly?' I would not know, but you mean at fly height yeah, that might be possible,' I said,' I mean what I say,' said my brother. I have had a very annoying way of walking for a while', he continued,' for example, I would no have been able to dance,' 'but you can do that now for me', he said. I must have looked haggard. I really could not follow him.' Okay Boy, feet off the floor', he cried, 'I want to see you dance.' Cowboy books in the wrong hands I thought. He is not going to shoot, I thought, I'll stand still and after a while it will blow over.

'Chicken boy', he now began,' show me the cans and I'll shoot them out of your hand or do a dance or I'll shoot you in the legs' That was straight talk, I held my hands with the cans on my back. 'Okay,' said my gun-loving brother, then it will be a dance.

No, I thought, I refuse, I won´t do a single step. It's all bluff, he would never be able to explain it. I should have said that, and not thought it. Many years later I would be in a course learning that you have to keep talking to misguided, dangerous idiots. He shot. Pieuw, the bullet ricocheted on the tile next to my foot and came up against the wall behind me, where it did some damage to the plaster work. I should have stayed, where I was, but I walked over to him. Pieuw, he shot again, some slivers of tile came against my leg. Now I stood still is, I should have kept walking. It was serious. I did jump up a little, I should not have done so. 'Higher', said my brother and shot next to my other foot. Just when I wanted to say that he was crazy, the next bullet off the floor bounced up and hit my leg next to my shin. The pain was like you got whipped.

'Ahhh,' I moaned and sank on the tiles as I looked at my leg. There was a hole in my leg. Grazed, I thought. My brother came back to his senses. 'No', he said' 'that was not the intention'.

'Sit down,' he said. I picked up the two cans and chucked them far away, 'I could do with a coke,' I started saying.. my brother squirted away, but took the gun along. He came back with two cokes. 'Hey', I said, 'where is my bb gun?' I have put in the bedroom, I thought that was better,' he said, and he was quite right. My leg really hurt, I dabbed it gently with a wet washcloth that my brother had brought me.

'This is between us,' my brother said. 'That might be but need not be,' I replied. However, I understood that he had hit me rather accidentally. It were power games that people feel, with weapons in hand. 'I think,' I said 'that it is sensible to do so.' Long pants!! My brother sprinted off to get to me my Jeans. Moments later we were reading fraternally together. My parents came back and it was a pleasant evening. An evening with a board games and stories. When we finally went to bed, my brother said to me, 'I am really very sorry. 'And I, Yeah, I thought I'd be very generous and I was, ' such things happen,' I said, 'we are even now, I think'. 'Yes,' my brother said and we shook hands solemnly.

The next day we got out late and we heard that my father, had been picked up by the van that brought the men to the airport. He had to go back for a few days to the desert. I still had a lot of pain and my leg pulsated. Suddenly I knew what was wrong, I had not heard the bullet strike the wall behind me, the bullet was still in my leg. 'Hey', I told my brother when I shook him back and forth, 'there is a problem'. 'What'? He still sounded very sleepy. 'The bullet is still in my leg.' He was immediately wide awake. 'You have shot me, you go and get it out', I said. He turned very pale. So we were a little later in the kitchen, my brother had a potato knife in the burner of the stove. Probably from a book, I thought wryly. He held it under cold water and began to move it about in the wound. 'Sit still,' he commanded me in a whisper. I tried to with all my force, but it was hard going.

'I see it,' he said suddenly, just when my mother came in. 'What's going on here', she asked? She saw my brother poking about with a knife in my leg and she saw that I nearly collapsed. 'Do not stop,' I told my brother who nearly froze when he heard my mother's voice. 'What are you doing,' she asked my brother? 'He is helping me,' I said, 'and I am glad he does, because I have shot myself in the leg' 'Get the medicine chest,' commanded my mother. After a lot of boric water and with the aid of a pair of tweezers she got the bullet out of the leg. My mother did not like half-measures, the iodine bottle came next and sulfa powder, then a bandage was put around my leg. She asked my brother to put the tea kettle on. When my brother gave me my cup, he said, 'thank you.'

The concubine

It was weekend and my brother had invited some Arab friends from his college. The beetles came whistling over the lane and stopped in front of our garden. Although it was a hot summer day, they came smartly dressed. They were dressed to a 'T. The suits were not bought but made by a tailor and fitted like a glove. They did not look hot nor flushed, and wore tie pins to keep their ties in place and cuff links that you could not help but notice. Blinking of gold. They tried to be American and only drank cola, they used brylcreme and took ketchup with every dish, but they could have come straight from a lecture in Oxford. They all used Old Spice aftershave and were confused.

They imitated both Americans and the British in an equally poor way. They confused the two status groups. Not surprising when you realize that until the second world war, Cyprus, Malta, and Egypt, and almost all Mediterranean areas, including Greece, had belonged to the British Empire, be it as a colony or protectorate area. Whether you saw

India or South Africa, or Singapore or Hong Kong, the British sceptre waved over many areas. My brother's friends used preferably American products, but they felt they had to dress like the British upper class. My father had vegetarian meals cooked and the table spilled over with small saucers with snacks. A couple of them walked approvingly around my brother's Ford. Their eyes went hungry, no other way to describe it.

They would open a door and then close it again. They leaned hard on the hood to see what the suspension was like and they were very impressed with the exhaust pipes. They absolutely drooled when my brother demonstrated the electric windows. They had windows that you cranked up or down manually, and the beetles had two doors, where the American tank had four large doors. If there had been no women in the house then the afternoon would have been flawless. There were discussions about politics and about their own homelands. Almost without exception, they all came from Lebanon and Egypt, and later they would do their utmost to raise the standard of civilization in those countries. The example that they invariably quoted was Saudi Arabia or Turky. In retrospect, we now know that they did not succeed They would have preferred to have belonged to the modern day Romans; the Americans or the Europeans. Their conversations showed the contempt they felt for the backward areas that were undeveloped, like Libya. Quite possibly they tried to flatter us, Caucasians, by intentionally criticizing Arabs. Arab people often have a double bottom, and after a time they will show it and speak their minds. Flattery is a very common in conversation, showing respect to the listener. They were educated, expressed their English perfectly, read British writers and discussed plays that they had read and probably would never see in real life.

One of the friends went to talk to my father and he claimed that he was one of the best friends of my brother, he was almost family, almost related to my father .. He began to name the possessions of his father's side of the family. I listened with amazement. The other students were talking in small groups and sat with cola or tea and ate civilized small bites of the waiting saucers. Achmet Ali, now began to praise the company where my father worked greatly and commended himself lucky that he was friends with the son of an expert who worked there. It would be his life's purpose may be to join that company some day. I got a picture before my eyes of the Arab men who had walked dunking in their boots to keep the flying foundation wet in the desert in the rain.

'I have two small gifts with me as a token of my gratitude,' Achmet Ali went on,' for inviting me today". That was not necessary,' said, my father, 'my son's friends are always welcome in my house'. He walked to his car and came back with two parcels in dazzling glitter paper. Would my father open it, I wondered or leave it for later out of politeness. Achmet took the lead and unwrapped it himself. It was a large silver or silver-plated hand of Fatima.

'The hand that exorcises evil and bring good luck. The hand was named after the daughter of the Prophet Muhammad'. My father praised the amulet exuberantly and it was beautiful, it was of very fine silver ornamental wrought work. 'I will hang it up in my house', he said with a big smile. 'It works better', said Achmet Ali, 'if it is given to you and you do not buy yourself'. He opened the second packet and out came a *Nazar*. 'You know what this is', asked Achmet, 'I picked it out myself for you.' 'I know,' said my father, who had always been very superstitious which was probably due to his childhood in Indonesia.' That is a *Nazar*, and everyone could see that it was a costly nazar. 'It is also called the Eye of Fatima' , continued my father. 'it wards off the evil eye.'Achmet beamed,' now my family is completely protected.' Was I the only one to notice that Achmet , called us his family now. You have honored us with your visit and you've outdone yourself with gifts that I myself would not have been able to surpass my father said.' You'll be my younger brother,' said Achmed to me. 'I already have a brother,' I said, and the moment of sweet magic and flattery, was broken. 'Before I join my friends, I want to tell you that I think you have a very graceful daughter,' said Achmet and gave a humble nod toward my father. I would like to talk to you and your eldest son tomorrow, if that suits you. I now knew what time of day it was' Achmet wanted my sister or something.

'Let's meet the same time,' my father said. Achmet Ali got up with a little bow and walked to another table. My brother immediately started, 'Dad,' he said,' Achmet is married and lives with his wife in his father's house in Lebanon. He has been married to her since he was 16.' 'We will hear him out tomorrow ,said my father,' I will ask Mohammed if he hangs up that mess'. Here my father spoke as his normal self again, this was his real face, no respect for anything that deviated from his norms. You could say a lot, but not that Achmet had given something that you could call a mess. The day passed and the next day a large model Fiat stopped in front of our gate and behind him Achmet came in his beetle. The Fiat man was presented as the uncle of Achmed. All the men sat at the table and I was allowed to join them, at least I was not sent away. My mother came out with tea and honey-sweet Arabic pastries, she put the tea down and disappeared into the house.'I have come here with my uncle to talk about your daughter,' Achmet began. I would like to ask if I may take her to my house as a concubine'. In any other country you would now have been beaten hard over the head by a raging father. 'What do you mean by concubine,' asked my father?'

'His second wife, 'explained the uncle.' His first wife is at home with my brother and his wife. Achmed is alone over here and that's not healthy for a man'. 'What is your role in this', my father wanted to know, eerily calm? 'I can vouch for Ahmed that his father will pay the dowry.' 'I can also testify that my cousin is serious, he wants to have children with a white woman.' Big deal,' I thought,' a lot of men would want children with my sister'. 'Have some tea,' my father said,' you surprise me a little with that question. I have to think about it and I want to explain to my family.' 'We are not without means,' said the uncle. 'That has occurred to me,' my father answered. 'Let's come together again next week,' asked my father, and he poured out some more tea.

The dowry

My father watched the two cars, until they were hidden by a cloud of dust they threw up themselves. 'Learn something from this boys,' said my father, they are from a different tribe than we are. They live in another time which is controlled by their ideas. They think in images that date from the time of their prophet Mohammed, who lived 1400 years ago, but they want to participate and provide guidance in our modern society. Without realizing it, my father had put his finger on the big Arab dilemma, it is to assert themselves in many areas in a modern time world, which does not reflect the worldly views of 1400 year ago. You cannot have a modern world that progressed in understanding, guided by laws or beliefs that are matched to the time of the Prophet Muhammad.

Where those worlds are kept separate, there is nothing to worry about, where those worldviews touch, prevails instantaneously misunderstanding and mistrust. A suspicion that quickly hardens positions and leads to fanaticism. The student friends of my brother, were in their world, respected men. In the eyes of the American companies, however, they were a bunch of suckers with good intentions. In the American and European community in Libya, people like my father and his colleagues enjoyed respect. In the eyes of the average Libyan, he was a Christian dog that had no business in Libya. 'Different tribes,' my father had said, and that described it unintended humoristic, but true to the core. We were not the same, we were no better, or worse, we were different and that held true for them as well.

The wealthy parents of the better circles that sent their sons to Tripoli to study, inadvertently destined them to a life of frustration, lost between two worldviews. After their study, filled with sacred knowledge and a diploma in their pocket which gave access to the modern world, they could begin by shying away from their roots. They became the pariah's in both worldviews. Modern man is a member of many tribes. A football club is a tribe, but so is a study group or a group of colleagues, a rock band. Some tribal alliances are temporary because you develop other choices. Place of your birth and your county or your birth determine unchanging relationships. In Libya, there is such an unchanging tribal connection. You are a Berber or not. A Touareg or a blue Touareg. Libyan leaders derive power from their kinship.The time has stopped, where it has proceeded elsewhere. Where the West with much trial and error, has attained a measure of freedom and prosperity, the Arab world still needs many trials and error. 'Let's go inside,' said my father. 'Beware', he repeated again, 'they are really different, you give them a finger and they take your arm. 'They cannot help that, it forms part of their being. They come with a hand of Fatima to see if there are other possibilities. They catch a glimpse of your sister and combine in their mind, possibilities. An entrance into my house, a relationship or advocacy to acquire a job and in addition enter into our race through the children born out of a union between your sister and them.'

I never heard my father this reflective. I saw the ratio or in what he said. Achmed doesn't know your sister, at most he has caught a remote glimpse of her. Immediately he sees in her a tool, a key, to obtain entrance through doors that will never open for him otherwise. He will have his way with her free rein and to him she will have no more value, and if there is a younger woman that comes along with other options, he needs to say only three times *Imshi*, which means 'go', and he is separated from your sister. He'll keep the children and the wife, used and broken is thrown away like dirt. 'So what was that all about', my mother asked my father? 'How many camels do you think your daughter is worth', was his reply. 'So there it is', my mother said.' He really wants to swap animals for my child', my mother was appalled. 'Not exactly, but it boils down to it.' He is more civilized and will not arrive with goats or camels, but it remains barter.' I understood deep in my heart how offensive it must be for a person to be traded for a few animals, a hand of Fatima, or a piece of land . Or what often happened, as payment of a gambling debt or a loan.' What a terrible country this is', said my mother. Don't people have rights here?' 'Women don't, in any case,' my father said.' But here we go. it is a nice fellow who wants to improve his position in the world.'

'If you reject him than he'll think because of his worldview, that you don't find him good enough. The honor is an asset in the Arab world. He's been so unwise to take along his uncle who has witnessed his proposal. If rejected, he will then know that his uncle, and also the father of Ahmed and the family of the father and his brother, will be affected. If we were only Arabic than it was one thing, but I, the father, along with my daughter, we are only white Christian dogs.

That really cuts into it. They all want a white woman and if they are rejected, then the girl is a worth-less, Christian dog whore.'

'He will also think it has to do with his skin color, and as it happens, right now, that is the farthest away from my considerations. He may become a very nasty man, if he is rejected. Generous Achmed with his nice gift, is a man from higher circles, with family members at high, probably purchased positions, civil servants. You should not be surprised if your light is cut off, or your visa will no longer be renewed, that sort of thing. Revenge to somewhat recover face'. 'What a nasty people anyway,' my mother said, 'I do not understand,' and she pointed to my brother, that you have brought these niggers in my house.'

Apparently she had taken over the ideas of my father acquired over the years about colored folk. Everything that was not white was a nigger. Nice for the Eskimos, albinos and the Chinese. I liked it better when they were referred to as other tribes, it came down to the same, of course. It has always amazed me that intelligent educated people talked in such a way about skin color, your color is only skin deep. More important is the mentality of people and whether they fit into your world view. Whether they want to understand your culture or are open to it or closed off. We sat around the table and ate a sandwich with some soup and I thought, what it would have been like for me to exchange my sister, for a motorcycle. Not to praise myself, but I realized that I did would not want to miss her not even for a chopper, my sister for a motor. Yet somewhere deep in my brains, there was a tiny part of me that thought, but... *a nice chopper*... I pushed it far away, so deep that it would never come to the surface again.

This is how these things work of course. If someone really wants something and a dowry can be achieved and the environment and culture find such barter quite normal, who are we to still continue with our Western ideas? The fact that there is a Dutch word for dowry makes you think. In a more recent past, there were dowries that changed hands, otherwise such a word would not exist in our language. 'I do not want to discuss this anymore,' my mother said, 'it is too ridiculous for words and the soup is getting cold anyway.' Thus the proposal of Achmed was descarted by the cooling soup of my mother. *Imshi Imshi Imshi, Achmed*.' 'We will use this week to consider of how to solve this all with honor.. Nobody should suffer harm. In any case, I do not want,' my father looked at my sister, 'you at home when the talk takes place next week. You will go for a few days to the American acquaintances.' For now, we all found that a good plan.

The dowry

The week had passed fairly quickly and my sister had gone to stay with acquaintances. It was late in the afternoon and the table was covered with delicious snacks. 'I hope that Achmed will be in time,' my father said, I do not want to lose the whole evening. My father and my brother were smartly dressed and I was with my mother in the kitchen. I was to be the waiter, when the guests had arrived. There was a squeaking and whistling and a beetle came to a halt. This time Ahmed and his uncle came in one car. There were bowls of dates and olives waiting on tables. The glass jug was ready, covered by a layer of condensation on the outside, with ice cold water. I walked up to them to welcome them and held the door wide open for them. The men both wore a white fez, as a sign that they had been on pilgrimage to Mecca, which is a sacred duty for all Muslims who are able to do so. They had come with big guns.

Inside were my brother and father waiting and the men embraced each other immediately after the greeting. An embrace that you see in hot countries without a second thought involved. My father pointed to two chairs and I in my role as a waiter rushed to pour out delicious cold water from the jug. The parties had come together. Achmed Ali looked around and I saw his face light up when he saw the Nazar, hanging where Muhammad had fixed it next to the door. His Nazar, hung next to the door to repel the evil eye. 'You know,' he started to have an opening, 'that if a Nazar is damaged one day, he has done his job.' Then he has kept away the evil eye. Then you can best replace him, because evil is always present" I am aware of that', my father answered. 'Every day when I leave my house I walk past your gift, and I see the goodness of your desire to protect my house.

'Achmed looked at my father and said, 'I will be pleased to accept you as a father.' ' A man has many obligations'. *Ihsha'Alla'*,. replied my father, which is an Arabic saying for, if God pleases, or if God wills it. My father had read the Koran, something many Libyans were unable to do, they depended on what an Imam explained in a Mosque . *Insha'Allah* is very widely used in Arab countries, it gives a projection of a desirability that you expect that will not take place and you put 110that decision in the hands of God. An Arab will not promise anything without adding at the end of his sentence. Insha'Allah.

It promises a high level of desirability, such as expressed in the Spanish mañana. Which does not necessarily mean tomorrow, but more: I like you and I do not want to do it, but I do not want to say that to you .. Where uncertainty exists this phrase is used, as in the Dutch adverb **perhaps** indicating that same uncertainty . My father had done well, in an Arabic way he had emphasized the desirability, but also had introduced the uncertain element of depending on God and God's mysterious ways. You cannot give those ways direction, that is only for the Lord to decide and do. At such moments, I was proud of my father and then I saw briefly a piece of his razor-sharp intellect.

Achmed was not stupid and took first some olives and a sip of water. My father took advantage of that opportunity to lay some packages on the table. 'It is good if a man thinks of his friends when they are not present,' continued my father. 'I thought of you both this week and I have brought something for you, so you can carry me and my home in your heart'. He picked up two packages and placed them next to the plate of Achmed. Receiving gifts is always fun and Achmed Ali looked longingly at the presents. My father now picked up the second package and gave it to his uncle. 'You are farther removed from my house than Achmed, allow me', my father said, and in boxes lay a tie of the Oasis company, with the logo of the palm trees and an oil drum, supported by the inscription, Oil and American technology.

An American tie! The uncle would rise enormously in prestige. He bowed his head and thanked my father. 'You', my father said, to Achmed, 'are closer to my house, let me,' and he opened the first package. American multinationals have a culture of management and accompanying ties. Like the captain on board the aircraft is recognized by his multitude of stripes as compared to the pilot, so there is a culture where management recognizes the ties in large American companies. At the door someone with a management tie will be immediately recognized and responded to accordingly. Americans are masters in management and organization.

The oblong box held a silk tie of the management of the Oasis company. *Um* was the logo, upper management.' Something to go with it,' my father said. He opened a box open and a gold tie pin emerged Sporting a small American flag and Achmed read the spelling, the print apparently was very small:' *I love America,*' he spoke with his British accent. It looked awful kitsch, bling and flashy. Achmed was beaming from head to toe. 'When you're done with your education next year,' said my father, 'look me up in the main building.' 'Show the doorman your tie and ask for me. I Will introduce you to my colleagues in the personal department and explain that you are a friend of the family, *Insha'Allah." Insha'Allah,*' repeated Achmed with moist eyes. I saw in my mind, Achmet, though ,walking through the desert with rubber boots and a waterhose.

'Garçon,' my father called, 'fresh water!'I rushed into the kitchen with the empty carafe.' How's it going in there,' asked my mother? 'It is about 10-0.' I replied. 'Dad is giving them a mental beating in a civilized manner. He has them almost numb.' 'Yes,' my mother replied,' that is as I know him.' I came into the salon to pour out water and Achmed was just done with a speech. He added to it, 'I do not know how I can thank you'. 'By doing my table honor, because on an empty stomach, men can not talk about weighty matters.' I hurried back to the kitchen and came back with a bowl of steaming chicken legs and then a bowl with filled eggs. Chicken is very popular in Arab countries, where it is seen as a clean animal.

Meanwhile, my mother driven out of her own livingroom was in in her kitchen reading a book. After a bite here and a dish there, the men were saturated. 'I have come today,' Achmed, began, 'to talk about your daughter with you'. 'I,' filled in the uncle, 'am here as a witness and as alternative of Achmed's father who lives in Lebanon and to control the Financial settlement with you. 'What about my daughter do you want to discuss,' asked my father? I'd like to count her as part of my household as concubine, Ahmed Ali simply said.. *Insha'Allah,* my dad said,' a finer son, a father could not wish for.'

'Have you waited long for a woman like my daughter?" Very long,' said Achmed. 'Then you will need to practice a little more patience,' continued my father, 'for she is travelling, with a chaperone of course'. Achmed looked crestfallen but pulled his face back into the fold. 'She should come to herself in time, she is in mourning, she has lost a good American friend.' Achmed Ali looked sympathetically across the table at my father. 'Do you know what a monastery is', my father continued? 'She is considering entering a convent. After her mourning period. ' 'A man alone is but one man alone,' Achmed replied, 'I do not know if I can practice as much patience but I will always look at you like a fatherly friend.' 'I know,' my father said, 'and if the situation changes, I will seek contact with you Insha' Allah.' 'Carçon, dessert', my father said imperiously, making clear that the rendez-vous was terminated. 'Total control', I informed my mother, 'he has just killed them'.

A bowl with sickly sweet honey cakes and coffee was served. The men got up and thanked us for the hospitality and walked out of our lives forever. I escorted them out and joined the others at the table.' Achmed is a very smart boy,' began my father' he has gained a meal, a management tie from me, a tie clip, and a wheelbarrow when he comes to apply for a job next year..' Furthermore, he is risen very much in his uncle's esteem, he is the coming man' 'Hmm, my father said, 'that can go in the bin', he looked at the nazar and pulled it from the wall. 'Why', asked my mother, just leave it there? 'On the contrary', my father said, and he held it to the light. There was a crack through the eye of Fatima. 'It just protected us against the evil eye,' my father said,' I'm going to buy a new one tomorrow. Immediately.'

National brotherhood week

The third week in February, is a week of great tolerance in America, then: national brotherhood week is celebrated. If you live in a country where every year a new wave of immigrants, must conform to a system that was already a melting pot of nationalities, then you need certain instruments to generate mutual understanding and you need to stimulate integration. In 1927, after a national conference between Christians and Jews, shape was given to such an instrument. A tolerance group formed, which had the following objectives: removing barriers between rich and poor, between people of different faith and their belief in creation, respecting each other's culture and ethnicity. A tolerance trio formed, a minister, a priest and a rabbi, who made thousands of miles, lectured and gave an impulse to tolerance youth camps. Dignitaries hooked on, especially those who had political ambitions and after many years a special week was born with attention to integration, national brotherhood week was a fact.

The OCs was a piece of America moved into the Libyan desert. Christmas was celebrated by putting up an artificial Christmas tree, which was taken out of storage, beneath it a large fake sleigh with a Santa doll on it, which looked a bit out of place with the desert sand around it. The Americans fl ew turkeys in on Thanksgiving Day and drew attention to the National brotherhood week. The entire third week was thematically marked by tolerance and understanding. Lessons were suspended and the school context was very different. You went to your homeroom and followed the customary rite of the pledge to the flag. Then the school anthem was sung. The history teacher had spent a lot of time on preparing stencils about the backgrounds of the Libyan history and spread these around the colleagues and the teachers had learned them by heart and were able to repeat them flawlessly. There was a satirical song over the intercom by Tom Lehrer, which was intended to encourage people to think and then followed two hours of focus on a subject and sounded that satirical song again over the intercom, to indicate that there was pause, Then came the satirical song again, indicating that you had to participate in the next lecture, and so it went on throughout the day.

The song was a satirical approach to brotherhood week, it was funny but would be politically incorrect nowadays.: National Brotherhood Week, we heard it that week so often, that it was cut into our thinking, I remember a few of the hard verses and I still must unconsciously snigger. Satire was wasted on my Texan classmates. They took the texts genuinly serious and sang lustily.

Oh, the white folks hate the black folks,

And the black folks hate the white folks.
To hate all but the right folks,
Is an old established rule.

Oh, the poor folks hate the rich folks,
And the rich folks hate the poor folks.
All of my folks hate all of your folks
It's american as apple pie.

But during national brotherhood week, national brotherhood week, New Yorkers love the Puerto Ricans' cause it's very chic.

Step up and shake the hand of someone you cannot stand.
You can tolerate him if you try.

Oh, the Protestants hate the Catholics,
And the Catholics hate the protestants,
And the Hindus hate the Moslems,
And everybody hates the jews.

The week started with a speech by the Principal about tolerance, which sounded tin like and distorted from the intercom speakers. He spoke about the greatness of America, a quality that found it's roots in the diversity of its population. The brotherhood week was important, he said, because you got to look at the similarities between people and not so much at the differences. You had to place Libya in a historical context, a context that was informative about its environment and its history, illustrating this he took an example that was less tactical regarding the brotherhood week.

He referred to the two wars between America and Libya, the wars took place in 1801 and 1804 and were known as the "barbary wars". Wars that were necessary, according to the principal as Libya had been an unrestful nest of hoodlums and pirates. Those wars still reflected in the anthem of the US marines; *from the **halls of Montezuma to the shores of Tripoli**.* It was an extraordinary speech where you started on tolerance and glorified the massacre of Libyan mobs by the Marines in a few sentences. He concluded by referring to cooperation, now, between America and Libya, where its technology was trying to achieve a prosperity through the exploitation of its oil resources, which would lead to a fortune for Libya and America and be an impulse of development for their backward areas and masses. The speech had been as tactical as the statements of an American president years later, who thought that Africa was a country. Let's just assume that they meant well.

The intercom buzzed and echoed the same brotherhood week song. *All the white folks hate the black folks and the black folks hate the white folks ...* Our teacher was talking about Tripoli. He had handed out a stencil least we were to read that in pairs and discuss it. Tripoli had been one of the three cities that were founded there in antiquity as it turned out, The **Tri** in Tripoli still referred to that. The towns had been **Leptis Magna, Sabratha** and **OEA**. They had been founded far before Christ by the Phoenicians. They had been settlements, along with Crete and Carthage, city colonies. I had never thought about it, but the cities were really very old. So **Leptis Magna** was founded in 1100 BC. **Oea,** nowadays Tripoli, in 700 BC and **Sabratha** in 500 BC. The Phoenicians were already off in 2500 BC in the process of building a trading empire around the Mediterranean.

The intercom buzzed and echoed the same brotherhood week song. **All the white folks hate the black folks and the black folks hate the white folks ...** *Oea* remained inhabited until the present day, the only one of the three cities, but the name Tripoli still refers to its two sister cities which became depopulated due to lack of drinking water. Oea has layer after layer of buildings standing over its previous civilizations, unlike Leptis Magna or Sabartha, which remained in original state, as pre Roman ruin cities left behind and part of the UNESCO heritage. Theme weeks are good, you will obtain very quickly bundled information. For example, we learned that the Arabic name for Tripoli was, *Tarásbulus al Gharb.* Which meant Tripoli from the west. It was founded by the Phoenicians who came from the area of Lebanon and Syria, which as a major city had a Tripoli. **Tarásbulus al-Sham** what meant Tripoli from the east.

We learned an incredible lot in the first two hours . The Phoenicians had first developed an alphabet and introduced money as bargaining means in trade. They called themselves the people of Canaan as in the Bible, but were known as the purple folk. That had to do with the fact that they like only people knew the secret to produce purple dye They dived fire horn snails up and broke open the shells and then squeezed hem so that they could win a few drops of purple liquid from a gland, You needed 30 000 snails to obtain 4 grams of pure dye. Very annoying, if you were such a snail, shall we say. However, I suddenly understood why the color purple had been the color of emperors and other dignitaries. It was the almost priceless color of power and wealth.

You were handed out a stencil and could answer the questions in pairs. For example, such a question was, why were huge piles of shells, of sometimes meters high, found during excavations at Troy and Crete, were they possible Phoenician settlements? If you had listened attentively then you knew that it might be pointing at the purple industry of that nation. The national fraternity song was played again by the intercom and we were increasingly aware **that it was okay to hate the right people. Alright to hate the right folks ..** A camel race was to be held, announced the intercom and in my innocence, I thought that there would be real couple of camels racing down our sports tracks. Nothing was further from the truth, those who had just learned about the ship of the desert in their classes could all sign up for the camel race. There were 10 participants selected from all the volunteers who had just learned to count in Arabic to ten **Wahed, Ithnani, Thalatha, Arbaha, Khamsa, Sitta, Saba, Thamania, Tisaa, Ashara.** They formed five pairs and had to stand with their legs tied together side to side. Now they only had three legs available. The righthand participant was also blindfolded. Everyone had to drink a water bottle empty. The sports teacher aligned the camels and counted to Thalata, three. You could not say they raced but there was acceleration of sorts, a cadence, staggering to the fi nish line. I must admit that their inelegant tottering walk, had really seemed camel like. On came the vocal message again from the

speakers that all the white folks hate the black folks and the black folks hate the white folks..en we knew we had to go back to the classroom again. Yes our teacher said you've seen it for yourself, a camel has a special trot and they drink themselves full before setting out. He showed his package of cigarettes, Camel it read, with a picture of a pyramid and a desert and a camel. What beast is this, he said, and he walked past as he held the packet up through the ranks. Who knows may say it. Clayton, a boy from Texas, raised his eyebrows and looked as if it was the stupidest thing ever asked of him and replied, 'that is a camel master' 'No,' said our master, 'that is unfortunately wrong.' 'Why is this not a camel' But Clayton, started,' it even says so on your package.' 'Clayton, a good advice if I can teach you anything in your life said our mentor, do not believe everything that is written. You may hand out the stencils.

Clayton went down the rows and laid on each table a stencil with the title: "The Camel" We read about the eating habits of camelis, their reserve storage of fat and moisture in the bumps. The routes they walked through the Sahara. There was information about caravan serais, which were a kind of protected overnight spots for merchants. 'Who has not finished it yet', asked the master. It remained silent. 'Good,' said Mr. Harper, more to himself than anyone else, 'Clayton look at this cigarette pack and tell me what kind of beast it is.' 'That, master,' said Clayton, 'is not a camel!' 'That is right, what is it,' the camels expert wanted to know?' I do not know, sir' said Clayton, 'but it is clearly not a camel'. 'Clayton', said our master who excelled in sarcasm, 'your wisdom exceeds your years, why is it not a camel?" A camel has two humps, 'our classmate replied, it says so in your stencil and the picture you have on your package is of an animal with one hump.''Brilliant', exulted Mr. Harper.'Clayton, so you gonna tell me that the producer of Camel cigarettes would not know what a camel looks like?' 'Or that master, or the stencil is wrong." I'm proud of you Clayton boy, you're even beginning to think abstract', said Mr. Harper,' the picture on camel cigarettes has not been right for years. A camel, as Clayton so rightly claims, has two humps and this beast', and he pointed to the pack, 'has one hump, and that makes him a dromedary.' I cannot believe it I thought, every week millions of packages are manufactured with a picture to support the brand and the image and brand name do not match. My thoughts were interrupted by a couplet which now came from the intercom that: **all the rich folk hate the poor folks and the poor folks hate the rich folks,** indicating that this lesson was over again.

It had been a special day and I walked to the yellow bus, filled with knowledge about the feeding habits of camels and the origin of Tripoli in my head. The bus where the fat Italian matron would push you about. It is alright to hate the right folks, I thought.

Leptis Magna

'Did you know,' I said,' 'that Tripoli has many names?' My parents were visiting friends and I was seated with my sister and brother at a table in the shade. My brother shook his head and my sister looked up in surprise.

'It is actually called **Oea,** 'I explained. 'That does not surprise me,' said my brother who was not very fine strung, 'that's monkey language.' 'No,' I said, 'that is actually Arabic or the Arabic that the Phoenicians spoke,' I said it', repeated my brother, 'monkey language.' I realized that my brother deserved five weeks brotherhood week, at least five weeks. 'What a funny name,' said my older sister, that does not sound like Tripoli at all and I made the observation that the social intelligence of my big sister was many times greater than that of my brother. It was a sweet sister and she would raise me like a second mother when the great disasters occurred in our family a little later.

'Did you learn that in school today', she asked? Yes, I nodded, 'and it is now called Tripoli because there used be three cities'. I have always had the unfortunate tendency to want to share knowledge. 'I knew that,' my brother said, 'everyone knows that,' he continued emphatically.' I for one, did not know that,' said my sister. 'What were the names then of those three cities,' I asked my brother. Who wisely not answered me, but asked if I had suddenly become very smart or a professor or something. I realized that he did not know and that he masked it in this way. I had a fun day at school and experienced much that was extraordinary and I just had to talk about it. I understood that you came nowhere arguing.

So I turned more to my sister and told about the camel race and history stencils and my brother listened and slowly but surely he began to ask questions. 'Which of those three cities was the oldest', he wanted to know?' Leptis Magna' I said without a doubt, I had read it on a handout. It was founded in 1100 BC, so 3,000 years ago. 'Holy shit and is there something left', he asked?' Yes,' I said,' very much so. Leptis Magna and Sabratha exist as nearly intact ruin cities.' 'How come,' my sister asked? They were abandoned by the drying up of wells and thus a shortage of drinking water. Oea as Tripoli survived because they had no water scarcity in that part. 'Would you be able to visit it,' he wondered? 'According to Mr. Harper, you can', I said.' He goes there sometimes, digging about and such, and finds nice things, a jug or something. "You can simply dig there', my brother watched me in disbelief. 'No one will stop you,' I replied, Mr. Harper had said that the British had even dismantled half a temple and shipped it to Belvedere, in Windsor Great Park, in London. 'We must go there,,' he said. I would really like that, I thought. 'Why can you dig there,' he asked? 'It does not interest the Libyans it is not their civilization that lies there.' 'Incredible,' said my brother, 'who knows what we may find there.' There was no Unesco at the time that would claim these places as cultural heritage.

In much later years a certain Colonel Gadafi mounted his artillery in the ruined cities knowing that the Americans would not bomb it. The ruined cities by now had been declared a World Heritage by UNESCO. My friends were asking me for a doebie game and that interrupted my lecture and a little later I was running about with my Arab friends in the made-up game. This was brotherhood week at top, not surprising because children also seek each other anywhere in the world and play without any prejudice.

That evening at the table, my brother began to speak about Tripoli and its old names. 'Oh,' said my father,' that was a Phoenician settlements of a few thousand years ago. They were a people that were called the purple race by the Greeks.

They squeezed dye out of snails. After the fall of Carthage, they rose very much in interest' and he took some rice. That was the end of it for him. I was impressed, I only knew since that morning how the fire horn snail was used to win dye. My father had such a different focus. He was so focused on technique that he took little note of other things, but in terms of their interest he immediately archived whatever he came across. He was pragmatic and technically inclined, there was nothing of the teacher in him. He was not a father explaining life to his kids gathered around him.

'Gosh, did you know Dad,' I asked?' Everyone knows that', replied my father and I saw the transit between my brother and my father,' it was clear to me they were both technical people and I came from another planet. My father introduced himself as the norm and anyone who didn't not know what he knew, was stupid. That is a curious form of modesty exercise and a huge underestimation of your own intelligence.' I did not know that,' my mother said and 'I would love to go there. 'Then you should go to Leptis Magna,' said my father, 'which is the oldest of the three and the most intact.' I almost fell backwards in surprise, 'have you ever been,' I asked him?' No,' he said, 'there's no need to, I know what there is to know.' 'However, I would really like to go', my mother said,' I want to see it with my own eyes.' 'It will be very hot now and the sun will really ref ect off the ruins and stones,' my dad tried. 'There, too, he was right, we knew later. 'We're going this weekend,' my mother said firmly.' I would like to do it for you, but my car goes into the garage for maintenance,' said my father. 'Doesn't your son have a car' and she pointed to my older brother. 'If he has no other plans,' my father said. That was not the case, my brother wanted nothing more than to go to the sites and so it was that we left Saturday morning for a ride of two hours to Leptis Magna. In the rear was a cooler with ice and drinks and we were all excited.

My father checked the water and the oil, even kicked the tires and we bounced down the path in the big Fairlane, followed by a deep rumble from the exhausts that betrayed the V8 engine *... **boh boh boh** .*.The road was bad but you would not expect otherwise, and after a few intersections and villages we came into a valley that ran down to the sea with only remaining pillars and ancient buildings. You had to leave your car because you could not possibly carry on. There were fallen pillars and debris of ancient temples. What you noticed was that you really walked into an old city. Of course, the streets were narrow, there was no other traffic at that time than a donkey or a horse. The Roman Forum was a joke in comparison. I had never seen anything like it and I understood that when we still walked around in bearskins, civilization had already been here.

It was impressive, as I was quite surprised that my father was a walking guide. 'Have you ever heard', my father asked, 'about Emperor Nero,' 'The emperor who fiddled while Rome burned?' 'He has built an amphi theater here somewhere that could accommodate 15 000 people'. We will look it up. Now, I know that it could accommodate 16 000 people, but for someone unprepared' my father was endowed with a lot of student's knowledge. There were young goat herds among the ruins and when they saw us, they came to us. They had some pots and shards and had found a handful of coins, which my father bought for a song.

There were two Americans at work with pick and shovel, there were some statues next to them and now I understand that something like that was criminal, then I found that very understandable. We passed triumphal gates, baths and temples. 'I will not move another step,' my father said while sweat was pouring down from him and he planted the cooler down... The heat reflected from every stone around us. We drank some and my brother and I asked if we could walk around a bit.' Stay in the field', my mother said,' I want to be able to see you' and so we walked a little later on a road that was older than the via Appia in Rome. We stopped once at a small pillar and we even walked past a piece of wall, but the truth is that the heat was overwhelming. It splashed on the roads and down the buildings, it was a natural oven.

You become very languid and you don't lift your feet well. The road we walked on was old, older than antiquity. It must have been a major thoroughfare in the ancient times, it was certainly wider than the other roads that were more like wide trails. I kicked a stone accidentally and it bounced forward and disappeared into a joint between two large stones that formed the pavement of the road. I had always been a good observer and I saw something out of the ordinary, the pebble was gone. 'Hey,' I said to my brother,' the stone is gone' 'Of course stupid,' he said,' you kicked against it'. 'I mean really gone,' I said. The joint was a gap of two inches wide. I sat down on my knees and threw a small pebble in, it took time and you heard a tick where it hit the bottom.

I froze,'we are above a vault,' I said, 'when it collapses we are done for.' 'Do not talk nonsense,' my brother said, but he also pushed a pebble through the opening between the two stones inside. I counted. 'What are you doing,' asked my brother? 'I am determining the depth,' I said. 'The gravity is 9.8 meters per second squared. So if you count the seconds you can determine how deep it is'. 'How deep is it,' asked my brother, 'who was very pragmatic'.

'Between 10 and 20 meters I guess,' I said. Very carefully we walked away from the edge. We realized that was the patchwork of old buildings with basements and vaults. We had lost the eagerness of walking around.

My parents and my sister were still recovering from the heat, and there were some pictures taken from all of us at a pillar here or a pillar there. Photos that I have now and cherish, one of the last pictures where my brother is still in good health, he was standing next to me, full of life and a smile on his face that the Emperor Nero could not have outdone . Back at the car, we saw it, it was obviously an American car, and it had been parked far away. The headlights were all shattered and suddenly we were back in the present, far away from the ancient beauty that we had visited. The hand of hatred searching through the regions had found us and squeezed the Christian dogs to rubble and searched for them and would bring them to harm, wherever possible.

the Waddan

Once a month, my mother and father went to the Waddan. It was a hotel, restaurant and had a casino. It was named after the antelope-like animal that still walk around freely in the desert with his curled horns and which was used almost everywhere in Libya as a national symbol. Even Wheelus, the American senior High School had it on their sports uniform, an image of the Waddan. My parents went there because my dad liked gambling. It was a weakness, one of the few weaknesses he had, but it was at once a very serious weakness. Occasionally, he had to give in to it. Lady fortune, was always around the corner waiting for him, if he lost his stakes then he could regain the lost money by playing 'just' once more and the money he had won in one month, he would lose twice in the following month. Real gamblers are superstitious, there is a sign that they only can detect whether there is a combination of the dice or the roulette table that will repeat itself. Later, when I studied economics and was plagued with probability calculations, it really dawned on me what a special assumption it had been for my father, to think that combination would be repeated with predictable regularity.

On the Saturday night of his gambling weekend, he went there a couple of hours around to note down numbers and combinations and then shared with my mother a nice dinner there and came home, he looked at his' tables', booklets of figures and numbers and combinations to identify the frequency data which only reveals itself to those who are addicted to gambling and belief in rushes of luck. Sometimes he had the "feeling" and indeed they'd come home smiling and my father would have won a lot of money. Sometimes the "feel" deceived him and then it was fortunate that my mother was with him and that there were no master cards at that time, because he would have come home penniless, he simply could not stop. it was a demon in him that he could not control.

We were not allowed to come along because you had to be 21 years old at that palace of gambling addicts, to be allowed to enter. To him it was not really about winning or losing, those who are plagued by the gamble demon, have an unconditional faith in lady luck and wait for that lady to reveal herself to them. As a kind of worship. They must participate in the entire ambience that gambling brings along . On one of those nights they came home delirious with joy. My father had experienced the 'feeling' and he had won £ 2500 at the card table, which was 25,000 guilders, at a time when a monthly salary in the Netherlands was 300 guilders, which were 7 years wages for a Dutch family. It goes without saying that within two months the casino had retrieved that money and even a bit more. This is when my father decided to safeguard us from that demon that would would play tricks on him until his death.

'So,' my father said, as he shuffled the cards, 'I'm the bank. The bank always wins, not immediately, but eventually it always will.' He played two trial games with us. My father, my brother and I were sitting around the table. My father probably assumed that women would never gamble. 'We will play Black Jack', my father said, 'it is also known as 21. You will learn it as we go along. Because there are still many additional opportunities that will present themselves while we play.' You had to get as close to the number 21 as possible. The bank had the advantage that they could keep one card upside down. Giving them knowledge that the opponents did not have. When you have 19 points in front of you, for instance, and you took a card from the bank which was a three, then you went over 21 points , and you lost your stake.

When nobody had 21 points, the player who came the closest won.' Suppose you all have two cards,' my father started off,' so there is one card from the bank open, which you can see. The other is to face down, face down. It could be that the bank has two tens, but only the bank knows that. It could also be that the bank has a ten and a two, face down, then the bank, has but 12 points, the croupier will then quickly look across the table and if there are players with higher points and their stakes are high enough than he will act on it. You have to think straight about the cards that have passed out and those that are still 'in' the game.' It seemed complicated, but after a few rounds, we believed that we were ready for the game. My father and my brother and I each had a pile of wine gums. After some games in which the bank often lost, we had a lot more wine gums than the bank. This was easy, I thought, it did not occur to me that my father as croupier might intentionally let the bank lose a few hands and massage a real lesson into us. 'Easy come and easy go,' I laughed, this would be a hefty profit if the stakes had been money for me, easily earned and easily lost for the bank. 'Gosh', my father said,' the bank has it's off days as well, it seems that you are having a lucky streak, a flood of happiness right from Lady Luck.' 'We'll take a break,' said my father, and drink and eat a bit. Don't we play anymore', I asked disappointed? 'Oh yeah' we will play for real, as men from the Casino,' laughed my father, if you dare to, at least. But that is only suitable for men who are not afraid and who laugh at their losses and never show how you hurt or what they think.' This has given me a lot of insight later in his acting, not showing what you really feel.

'I'll lend you some money,' he said, and put some coins on the table. 'Sign over here, this is serious and a piece of paper ,but worth what you sign for', we put a scrabble below the coin amount. After a few games, my brother and I were already in the profit. 'Nicely done.' said my father, 'what you had signed is called an **IOU**, that comes from what **I owe you**. You should never play with it, because then you play with money you don't have, with borrowed money. Never play with checks or borrowed money. We both nodded very seriously. Let's just redeem your IOU,' suggested my father. We pushed the coins that we had borrowed forward. 'That's not enough,' my father said, 'the bank always calculates interest'. Now we lost. almost all coins.

Does not matter, my father said, 'you did not go in the hole, but you could have.' 'Will we really, really, make it interesting,' my father said, 'we can play for your pocket money. But I will not lend you money anymore, no more IOU's, you are inexperienced players and have no credit with me'.

'But how can we play,' asked my brother? 'Don't you have piggy banks, then,' my father answered. 'I want to play with you, but only if you want to.' I pitied my father, the bank, we would clean him out, we were so lucky all afternoon.' I play', I said. 'Me as well.' added my brother, and here began one of the most painful lessons my father ever taught me.

'You have to keep some spare money apart,' my father said. 'I want to play a total of no more than 2 pounds with you and in small coins.' 'I happen to have a lot of change,' I now suppose that was no coincidence but a carefully planned scheme, which would unfold itself as everything my father did, methodological, step by step without failing. There we were in the home casino, Casino Royale. It was not long before we were broke. Suddenly the bank won a lot of rounds and played more than professional. We were stripped. I had lost a quarter of my total capital of 8 pounds savings money and I thought what every gambler thinks, but what if I had more money. .. because .. luck might change.. A little later, in about three more rounds a I had nothing left and my brother went broke.

'Thank you gentlemen,' my father said, and put the 4 pounds in his wallet. 'Hey,' my brother said, 'it was a game, right?' 'No,' my father said, 'the bank does not play games.' You have really played and you've really lost'. it was a lesson that would cling to me for life and never have I taken a seat at a gambling table or a card table. It is better if you lose a quarter of your capital on your thirteenth than at forty years old. It was a hard lesson. My stomach still turns to when I see people throwing money into a slot machine.' Fools,' I'll think, you are throwing your money away, but you have to know that the pay ratio 70 to 30 of every hundred percent, only 30% will be paid and distributed over many turns to keep the people eager. My father knew all those things and gave us a lesson so that we would not even consider ever to gamble. Too bad my grandfather had not done so with my father.

When we were there at the verge of wailing my sister came to tell us that a gentleman had walked up to our house. We got up. It was the servant of Achmed, the man who had asked my sister as a concubine. 'Peace on your house', the man greeted us with a little bow,' I have a message for you from my master.' It was an envelope which he held out. *To my benefactor friend*, it read on the outside. *You are invited to the feast of men, the second day of my intended marriage. Location: the Waddan, please confirm whether you will, present that to my servant.* My father looked at us and said, 'our friend Ahmed takes a concubine for himself and invites our presence at the feast of men.' 'We will go', my brother said, isn't that so, Dad?' 'Yes,' my father said, 'we will honor him with our presence' and so the servant of Achmed left moments later our house, to notify his master that we had received with joy, knowledge of his proposed marriage, and would participate in the celebrations. 'That means,' my father said, 'that no one goes to school tomorrow, you will go with me to the tailor to have a suit measured.'

'But we have suits,' my brother said. 'No', said my father,' as a future colleague of mine gets married, than we are not going in used clothing. The eyes are already focused on us, as non Arabs, as whites that are present.' So it was that a day later that the tailor took my father's and my brother's measurement for a few tuxedos. I was to get a suit that my sister scornfully called 'a Pipo the clown' suit. It was not checkered in that sense, it was a quite fine pepita speckle that ran through the fabric, but the fact that my sister had called my suit, ' a Pipo the clown suit', was enough to never want to wear it. It was a tailor-made suit and fitted me like a glove, but the comparison with Pipo the clown was too much at an age when it is very sensitive to ever to put the suit on without a previous battle. The, '*Hey*' she had said, 'look at that, **here comes Pipo the clown**', was enough to mark me for life. The power of the word with the sensitivity of the age caused me to struggle until I grew out of the suit, which fortunately did not take too long. I still do not buy checkered Bermudas.

Djellabah's and milk

My brother and my father looked like a parody of James Bond, my father, an obese James and my brother too young a James. The tuxedo's looked well on them though. I myself wore my Pipo suit and the more my mother and my sister assured me that my suit looked great and I did not look at all like the famous clown, Pipo, not even in the slightest; the more suspicious I was. As we drove to a party, an Arab party. I had a vague feeling of tension and expectation. I had no idea how the evening would go. My brother told me that his Arab peers were all invited and that the family of Achmedas had rented a large part of the Waddan.

We saw it when we drove up, it was very busy, the guard who was standing in the parking lot with the barrier, saluted us and let us through. The parking lot was filled with all kinds of nice-looking cars, and a few beetles. What you immediately noticed was that the clothes of the guests was different from ours. Many men wore *Djellebah* over their costume. That immediately made us feel naked. The Djellebah's had not just been chosen at random. They were all white and reaching just above the ground. A kind of garb that a priest might wear. in the Western world. Some had instead of a costume, more traditional clothing, a Dejellebah with underneath a white shirt and white pants. But everything was flawless and dazzling white.

We were kindly greeted by some fellow students from Achmed and my brother. They all touched their hearts and lips and forehead which I still find a lovely greeting. You feel no evil, speak no evil, and you think no evil of your friends. A nice smooth and symbolic gesture. They looked like princes from an Arabian fairy tale. Everything in Arab countries is focused more on image than is the case in Western parts of the world. They were white to their pointy shoes, and a few of them had white curled 'Aladin' slippers on their feet. Clothing stores in Tripoli had enjoyed a good week, that was for sure.

We walked with Arab friends to the main entrance. We stood out clearly without our white robes, maybe we could have informed ourselves in advance but because of the Western arrogance and complacency we were punished once again. Everywhere you saw happy people preparing to attend a party, friendly looks, nods and hugs and hands being shaken and it was a widening feeling of joy that pervaded through the multitude which increased in number and, slowly went in through the wide glass doors. As you got closer you could hear the traditional music whirl in the quarter notes, with floating melodies that you hear only in Eastern countries. A horn-like instrument with accompanying hand drum and reinforced by a violin was played in a way that you just do not hear anywhere in the West.

Specifically, It made me think of a record my father had, with gypsy orchestras and on it a violin played very different to anything I had heard before, feverish, whipping up a melody and a rhythm that would continue to haunt you. The music was getting stronger as you approached the entrance. Now you could observe the musicians, they were in traditional attire, seated with crossed legs on a platform. This was not an orchestra but just a traditional welcome. I suddenly felt ashamed for the many Americans whom we knew from school and my father's work that had such low derogatory opinions about anything that did not come from Texas.

All of the sudden I felt ashamed of my brother who always spoke disparagingly about crotch scratching Arabs, our guardian, who called every Arab, a Mo, I was ashamed that I was not an Arab, and yet was allowed to be present. What a rich culture implicitly enclosed in that enticing music and those present who were genuinely happy, without a drop of liquor consumed, simply happy because of a party. Now it became clear what delayed the influx so much, there were servants with trays full of small glasses and saucers waiting and each guest took a glass and sipped it and ate a bit. Abath a friend of my brother's study, with his British accent who could have walked around at Oxford any day of the week without being noticed asked me, 'do you know what happens there?' 'No,' I said, but I found everything simply stunning.

'We take a date and a glass of milk'. I went pale, I really could not stand milk.' I have a problem with an enzyme in my stomach,' I said, if I only smell milk, then I have to throw up'. 'Then do not smell it, he said, 'but just moisten your lips and wipe that off later. The date is the wish for fertility and milk is the purity of the bride.' 'Yes,' I said suddenly a little worried. 'It is about the desire,' he said.' Do you really have a problem with milk,' Abath wanted to know? 'Yes,' I replied, very much so, ever since I was little'. 'I'll help you then,' he said. Again someone who was very civilized but would have been called from a distance by our guardian, a Mo..The glass was small, it was more about the symbolism, a small saucer with dates was waiting. I took the glass and held my hand around it so that it was almost hidden in my neighboring fingers, I held my breath and brought it to my lips until I felt the fluid touch my lips and I let my hand down again.

Abath gave me his glass which was empty and drank mine in one gulp empty. We took a date and now walked along the welcome ensemble. In the distance we saw Achmed, he gleamed and smiled from ear to ear, the happiness splashed off him. Beside him stood an impressive appearance, 'that is his father,' reported my brother, 'I have stayed in Lebanon in his house. I'm going to greet him' he said, as we walked, followed by Abath and the others towards Achmed and his father.

His father stepped out of the family line and pressed a kiss on the forehead of my brother, a heartfelt kiss. 'Almost son of my house, 'he said, I've been expecting to see you, what a day of joy.' 'This is my father,' my brother said. 'Pleased to meet you,' said the stately man in his posh robe and he turned back to my brother. 'We've missed you', he continued,' you know the way to my house , now don't you,' and I just had the feeling that it was meant sincerely. 'Later I will still speak to you', he said, 'there are so many friends that are to be welcomed'. I thought him to be a very nice man,' said my father, who in this circle had no value. His personality was totally eclipsed by the collective of thousands of years of customs and culture.

There were snacks, incredible appetizers, all made with care. Two uncles of Achmed took my father under their care and I walked with my brother and his friends through the enormous hall. 'Are there no women', I asked Abath? Who said, 'yes, of course there are,, they are waiting in another room. 'I realized, they had really laid out a small fortune, if there were about as many women in a different hall, than you were talking about hundreds and hundreds of people. 'What are they waiting for,' I asked? 'The bride of course,' said Abath. Then they come out and we carry her to her room. 'Well', I thought,' it seems all a bit strange to me but I'll see what happens.' I had long forgotten all about the bride, our group ran walked around just like the others with a hot drink in our hands or a delicious spicy meat snack, You only had to look up and a servant of the Waddan would appear, with a tray. It was cozy, there was a huge buzz. Unnoticed the hours passed. The doors opened and out of the other room ladies walked to the entrance. A man went to the door with a horn, followed by a man with a hand drum and a stringed instrument ...

The drum rang out accompanied by bells on it, it was rhythmic, uplifting. 'The bride is coming,' whispered Abath and friends nodded. Suddenly the musicians stopped and they stepped aside. There a party came striding in. The man with the horn blew one blast and stepped aside.

In the banquethall we all went a few steps forward and then formed a crescent. The bride walked forward, covered with jewels and draped in a beautiful dress. She looked sad and every few steps forward, she paused with her gaze fixed on the ground and then she turned around and looked longingly at her family and friends who were moving away. I understood the symbolism, like lightning it hit me. The parting from her family to a new life, to another life as an adult woman, you no longer sit at your parent's table. 'Is she not happy,' I asked Abath? 'Yes, of course she is happy,' he replied, she just shows that she has had a quite happy childhood.

Achmed stood beside his father with arms spread open, but did not move. 'Here come the *Negaffa*,' said an Arab student. They came forward from the ladies hall. They surrounded the bride and made imploring gestures with their fingers as they cried out all kinds of words to the bride. 'What is taking place', I asked my Arabic teacher? 'They are making gestures of happiness and wish her health and happiness.' What little do we Westerners know, what a lot we have lost in our modern development to a stressful life. They carried her to a kind of throne and there she took place. The music began to play an insane cadence and strong men lifted the chair and walked her through the banquet room above their heads.

Other men walked up to Achmed, and lifted him up. Adored he went, up in the air The music was now downright insane in its intensity. Occasionally, the sedan came near Achmed and passed on hands, he was transported through the hall. Leaping through space Then everyone paused and the bride touched with her hand the groom as a sign of their covenant to be. Then back into the flow they were carried. Just as suddenly as the music had started, it stopped. Achmed came to stand back on his own two feet and the bride disappeared with her throne, into the ladies hall.

Meanwhile it was midnight, and now came the warm dishes, poultry and fish dishes steaming and surrounded by rice and spicy side dishes. There were no set places and you sat and ate delicious food and it took hours, there was no rush. The tables were cleared and the men went to the middle and a dance began, a dance that you followed, until you fell over. Some men had contact through a white handkerchief which they held between them. Every time the music started, a new dance began. A moist heat began to arise in the hall.

I saw my brother standing next to my father watching, they'll never learn, I thought as I swirled along with some men, and later with arms around each other behind the backs beating the ground with a few steps to the left and then again a few steps to the right followed by a stamp on the ground and back a few steps forward. Followed by a stamp on the ground and back a few steps to the left in an endless repetition of time that passed. These men knew what celebrating meant. When the music stopped, the table had been set again in the meantime and Achmed got up and pulled his djellabah off. A friend came rushing up and gave him a spotless white jacket. He looked around and happiness radiated from him. With two hands, he touched his heart and pointed in all directions. His gaze also rested on us for a second.

The man with the horn came forward again and blew a shrill blast. The door of the women's room opened slowly and the bride had changed, she had a beautiful white Western wedding dress and came in floating straight to Achmed and took her place beside him. 'Note,' Abath said, 'this is about the dowry.' The father of Ahmed came forward walking with his brother and the father of the bride came walking up with a family member. The two fathers did not speak. The uncle of Achmed raised his voice and asked loudly, 'have we complied with the dowry' 'Yes,' said the man next to the father of the bride, 'more than required. There was much rejoicing and the two fathers went to each other and fell into each other's arms'. Two waiters now came in and pushed a trolley with a whopping big wedding cake on it, to the centre of the hall.

The bride and Achmed held the knife, cut off a piece and gave each other a bite. The music started to play insanely, the guests were clapping and cheering, others made photos and Achmed and his concubine strode away. 'Where are those going,' I shouted into the ear of Abath. 'To a private party with the family in private.' It was half past six in the morning when the cake was gone and coffee had been drunk, the guests left the hall slowly but surely. We drove in silence back to our home, we all had a lot to process.

Europe around the corner

The British had always appropriated very strategic places, Malta was one of those places. Malta with a few islands around her was British and remained so until the '60 's. It was about halfway Gibraltar, the passage between the Atlantic Ocean, which was also British and Suez in Egypt which was a British protectorate. It was after the completion of the Suez Canal in 1869 that Malta grew in importance. It then became an important place for the British to obtain supplies on their way to India, their crown colony. Although the British were against the Suez Canal first, because Egypt wanted to offer access to all vessels under any flag and thus competition was concerned with trade in India, the canal however was later regarded as a technical triumph and blessing. The British government tried with Stephenson, to stop the canal by constructing a railway from Cairo to Suez, but progression cannot be stopped.

The canal was dug in ten years by a total of 1.5 million workers, including thirty thousand slaves and became a success, although many slaves died. It shortened the travel time drastically to India and Indonesia. Now ships could take a shortcut from the Mediterranean to the Indian Ocean, instead of sailing around the whole of Africa. It was progress, but not as innovative as one might assume. As it appears now, pharaoh Senusret II who lived in 1800 BC, had a connection dug between the Nile and the Red Sea, thousands of years earlier. It should be noted, however, that the Red Sea was not so withdrawn as it is now and not as far inland. Here, too, slaves were used, there is not much new under the sun.

Malta was the last European stop on the way to India. It was also with its 300 kilometers from Tripoli, a part of Europe that was enticingly close to us. My father rented in the hottest days of summer in Libya, a house in Malta. In distance it was not far, you flew to Malta with a British company, BEA, within an hour, in a roaring, deafening propeller plane. But although it was not far away in terms of distance, it was worlds away from Libya. So it was with some delight that we heard from my father that we would go again for a short stay to Malta.

My sister and my mom found it particularly great. They would be able to walk in the street and go shopping. My brother and I thought of the Italian influence and of pizzas and other European blessings. you could just eat ice cream without getting. typhoid fever. You could go anywhere, buy all kinds of magazines and return to Tripoli laden with paperbacks.

Everyone spoke English and you would be able to read every label. People are language animals and if the inclusion of language is disrupted then you cut them off from an important social vein. The Arabic script differs from anything we had ever seen, it would be refreshing to be able to read each billboard. It made you part of a society where you have control over your environment, because you understood everything.

'Where are we going to live,' my mother asked?' I have arranged a house', replied my father, 'in La Valletta, the capital'. That seemed pretty amazing to us all. That was close to the harbor with the British fortress and a park that ended with a fenced cliff, where you whizzed down with an elevator. The streets were filled with ordinary people. The hand of hatred that wanted to squeeze any non Muslim to grit, would remain in Tripoli. We would not be spat out where ever we went and feel hated. 'It's only for a few weeks and I'll just fly there and back for my work as needed' my father said. We knew from experience that we would not need much. Just some shorts and a vest for the evening just in case. Whatever you came short, you could just buy, you could just buy anything what you wanted! There were shops and bakeries and grocers and everyone was friendly. I now know that everyone was just normal and that the Libyans were simply unfriendly to anyone who was white.

Thus passed the last days at school and it was one of the last evenings we ate at the table that my brother said, 'something strange has happened today at the college.' 'Oh,' my father asked, 'no problems I should hope?' 'No, not that, but something that I feel rather uneasy about,' replied my brother.' Two boys in my class and I had weird notes under the windshield wiper.' 'What do you mean weird notes,' asked my father?' I have it with me,' answered my brother and pulled out a folded note from his wallet. *American Satani, we kill you,* it insisted in awkward writing. 'This was written by an Arab', my father said immediately.' The writing leans back. Left to right. Someone who's used to Arabic writing. It was not written by a student, then it would have been flawless. It was supposed to be: we will kill or shall kill you. That holds a future promise. 'What is a Satani,' asked my sister?'

That is Arabic for devil or demon', my father answered. 'It's an untrained and uneducated hand that wrote this,' was my father opinion, 'you cannot do anything about it.' 'Were the other notes the same?' 'Yes,' my brother said, 'the other boys are from Lebanon and they found it on the windshield of their beetles '. 'Envy and hatred,' my father said. 'Your car is typically American, so they probably thought it was the teacher's car.' 'The other notes, I don't like,' my father said. 'Someone is keeping an eye on your school and knows that those beetles do not belong to Libyans.' It's xenophobia.' 'Probably someone who thinks that Arab boys should not go to an European / American College.' 'I've seen this before,' my father muttered, with a faraway look. 'Keep your car locked up well', he advised my brother, 'so that some misguided idiot does not throw a scorpion or a snake in your car.

I felt a shiver creep up my spine. Nothing happens without a reason, times were grim, I knew so. A hand or perhaps in the meanwhile hands of hatred, went through the streets of Tripoli and looked for Americans or whites in general or for the Christian dogs and they would squeeze us to a pulp, we had no chance, I felt it deep down. just and a little later I shook it off me and we made new plans for Malta. Had it been a hunch? If someone or something could channel that hatred, we all lived on borrowed time, Men, or someone, knew or observed us, in which car we drove and felt strong enough to threaten and intimidate us. Would they know where we all lived, would they put lists in the hands of extremists. Even more than just for the sake of holidays, I wanted to go Malta. It were wonderful weeks, it would be the last holiday that we would enjoy as a family. Together in health. Luckily we didn't know that, or otherwise we would have gone bent under grief, years earlier.. Was it when we left Tripoli a few years later, that the hatred, had stuck to us forever, always surrounding us and had it followed us from far away, as fate haunts and destroys at times, because evil sticks to you and your fate will not let you escape your destiny? I do not know, but if I could have imagined that some of my family members were living on borrowed time with a clock that slowly, already started counting down their last few years, than I would have enjoyed those days even more with them.

My father rented a car and the steering wheel was on the wrong side, Malta was British and the cars and traffic were adjusted to the right side of your car. You did not look first to the left and then to the right if you wanted to cross a street, but you had to do the exact opposite, or you'd be knocked over or killed by traffic. That was an experience! We woke up and my father played opera music, we had breakfast and packed a picnic basket and went to a beach. So we lay on the beach of Golden Bay and my sister and mother could just lie on the beach, just like all other people. Another day we'd go to St George's bay of St Julians Bay and it was always nice and fun and the time was infinite and my brother and I would walk down the street when we came back home from the beach and we thoroughly enjoyed ourselves. We had to be home for dinner. Not that my mother cooked. We utilized the luxury that you could go to all sorts of restaurants, which was impossible in Tripoli, because they were simply not there. Everywhere were bistro's or pizzaria's, it was unbelievable!

With our Libyan pocket money, we just could not spend our money, everything was so inexpensive. For my father with his Libyan pounds and petrodollars, Malta was dirt cheap. Oh, life is so relative. We enjoyed Malta so much, because it had everything that Libya had not, or would ever have, freedom! Freedom in the European sense of the word. My father left us for a while to work in Tripoli and made us members of a complex called Villa Rosa, it was on a bay and looked like the Underwater club in Tripoli, with the difference that it was far more luxurious. My brother was not allowed to drive with his Arabic driver's license in the Maltese car. So we took the bus, which cost virtually nothing. We would go to Sliema and the old bus, painted green, moaned as it ascended the slopes, toiling, with a ticket seller who was in a separate cubicle... There was a bus! In Tripoli, you did not have any. The days became one happy event and we truly enjoyed them. My sister and my brother and I formed a trinity, I loved them so much and the days were great.

My father came flying in again, and the day after, he hired a speedboat and we flew on wings of power over the water with a bow wave that fled away from the boat and the sun tanning us. There were some drawbacks in the water around Malta, they swarmed with sharks, they just swam into the harbor and ate up the mess that the ships discharged. You often had a shark guard at the beaches who just hour after hour scanned the horizon for the dreaded fin, which would split the water open and people in it. 'Shark', such a man would roar, and then in a flash everyone was on the beach.

Beaches were not yet shark protected with nets or fences. It really was invested with those beasts. I had never been aware of it, until then, but the Mediterranean is a shark paradise. My father made us promise not to go into the sea any deeper than our waist and that we always had to make sure that we had people around us, so in case of sharks they'd be eaten and not us. We lived that summer exuberantly and if there is a God, then he has been gracious to us, that he had granted us those last great carefree days.. together.

Everything comes to an end and the new school year approached, the leave period expired. 'We will visit tomorrow something special,' my father said, 'and the next day we will f y back to Tripoli.' Everything was so special was that we were very curious. 'Tomorrow,' said my dad, 'we'll go to places that you will never forget'. One was called Hassan's cave, where a pirate had lived who had had his base there and the other was called the Blue Grotto, which you could sail into with a favourable tide, as the entrance was quite low. They were both really unforgettable places. Hassan the pirate, appealed very much to my brother's and my imagination, which made sense at that age and the Blue Grotto, was a natural wonder. The water was blue, a heavenly blue, and if you pulled your hand through the water, it appeared bluish as well, it was a combination of minerals that caused it, the cave was what it was, a beautiful place on this earth. The engines sputtered and the propellers started to spin around and cut their way through the air. My sister and my mother were dressed or covered up again in the Tripoli way.. Moments later the Bea plane landed at the airport in Tripoli and taxied to the steel plated hangar that would be hot like an oven. There were steps pushed to the front door and moments later we were standing on the platform in the heat that reflected in all directions. We had forgotten, for a few weeks what Libya was like , but now we were back 'home'. Malta, seemed far away, a stored memory, we were back in another world. Malta was far away, so very away from us.

We drove back in my father's car and when we arrived at our house and the yard, we saw that something was wrong, very wrong. Where my brother had parked his car, a few weeks ago, there was only a burned wreck now, resting on the rims. 'No, 'my brother cried aghast and held his hand over his mouth and I knew it, we were back home. The hand of hatred had sought street after street and found suggestively our street. The hatred full of suppressed anger had tracked us and had only for a moment, just slightly, pinched the Christian Dogs pinched as a promise of what lay ahead them.

Grim times

My father and my brother were busy for weeks with the insurance company of the Ford, which had now been towed to a garage. At some time an expert would come and together with the owner they would determine the damage. Burnt out, it stood in a parking area next to the garage, a sad reminder that looked nothing like the shiny car it had been a few weeks earlier. 'Can I see the papers and check them' the man had asked, who had come to our home. My father gave him the stack of papers. It were the original American papers and papers involving importing the car and changing it to Arabic plates. 'I will take care of it,' the man said, who was Arabic, but spoke fluent English and without the slightest trace of an accent. He wrote a phone number on a piece of paper and said, 'if you still have not heard anything within two weeks, call me. We are very busy with this type of incident'.

The next day the school bus with me in it, drove past the garage, I saw that the parking field was empty. Finally a firm that take clients serious, I thought. It was the last year in Junior High School. The O.C.S. ended with grade 9, then you could complete the last 3 years at Wheelus airbase, at senior highschool, which ran until the 12th grade, and then you got departementals. These were the school exams that gave you access to universities. That was if you followed the matriculation program, which I did. You could also get through High School by accumulating credit points that you earned, doing sports or typing and a bit of arithmetic, you only needed 100 credits, then you could not study, and you had a blank diploma. Then you had finished your school career with a high school diploma, but you could not do anything with it.

I looked forward to it, I had three years to determine what I would study, without a shadow of a doubt I would study later, everyone else was going to. I was thinking of something with science, the natural sciences and in it I preferred biology. I also really liked literature and thought I could take it later as a minor subject. It never occurred to me that this choice would be an odd combination.

We had already begun preparations for graduation exercises. Occasionally the group that was to graduate, met and then you had 142to stride forward on piano music in the auditorium. They were dry exercises. We all were assigned a partner with whom we had to walk forward. My partner's name was Gail and naturally came from Texas and was really pretty. Now I understand that we were selected, as Americans organize their affairs really well, alphabetically.

We had to finish our days on the OCS. Some would not see each other after graduation, because their fathers had taken on work elsewhere. Little did I know that no one would see each other after graduation, we would all be blown away, fleeing from a war that crept closer, but no one realized that. The bus then entered the parking field throwing up clouds of dust and the Italian lady worked us out of the bus, which interrupted my flow of thoughts. At home, I announced that the Ford on the field, was gone. My brother thought that it would not be long before we would hear if it would be repaired or would be written off. In the policy it had been insured against fire but what if the fire had been lit, I wondered? Should we not have reported that there had been a fire somewhere? 'You have no idea,' my brother said,' fire is fire!' That seemed to make sense. No one had seen anything, which was strange though. The coin fell, there must have been a neighbour of course, who had seen something, but wanted nothing to do with it. Perhaps Muhammad, our gardener had watched it from a distance, without intervening. When the rubber tires on the rims were burning away, it must have given a lot of thick smoke, someone must have seen that. Was I the only one who thought this?

That night at the table, my father said that he would not go to his work the next day, but that he would go for an examination in the Mossad hospital, with my mother. I took that for granted, but my sister asked, 'what sort of examination?' In foreign countries family members depend more on each other, and there are not many secrets. My mother answered my sister,' I have a lump in my breast and I think it has grown'. I did not know what could cause such things, but it seemed right and natural that you would then go to a hospital. My sister frowned but said nothing. The next day came and passed, and when we came home, my father said, 'Mr. Tidwel is coming soon, he will stay here for a while.' That was fun, it was a nice man and, in the event that something would happen to my parents, he would act as our guardian He had taught me a lot about stones and arrowheads.

'Why,' asked my brother?' I'm going with Mom to Malta, tomorrow,' my father answered and we'll stay a few days. 'How come,' I asked. 'The Mossad, Dr, Ledford has referred us to his colleague, Dr. Francis in Malta. He thought that the hospital in Malta was better equipped and more European." What will happen then,' I asked worried? 'Dr. Francis will make a small incision' and he saw my questioning look. 'He will take a piece out Mom's breast away and examine that in a labaratory,' he explained, 'that's really necessary, otherwise we would not do that.' I nodded but did not become much wiser. It was good that Mr. Tidwel coming enlightened the atmosphere a bit, but that night was not a night at the table with laughter and fun stories. Everyone was worried. I did not like the idea that someone would cut into my mother, but everyone avoided the subject.

Those were fun days with mr Tidwel, he made a lot of jokes and I now understand that he did it to divert our attention. He took us to the bowlerina, which was a kind of bowling alley and tried to teach us the intricacies of bowling at and now looking back, I think how lucky we had been, with the good friend he was to my father. The days passed and after the fourth day my father's car entered the yard and I flew out to meet them. My mother got out smiling and I hugged her. 'Calm down boy,' she said,' or I will fall over'. My brother and sister were at an age when you show your emotions less but they also kissed my mother. I looked at my father and he smiled down at me, in those days he still loved me. We walked in and like my mom was, she had bought presents for everyone. We sat down around the table. 'And big Dan,' asked mr Tidwel?' We will know within only a few days. They will call me at the office if Dr. Francis knows anything.' ' A bit of tissue is being examined,' my father explained to me. We want to know, if what is taken away, is benign or bad.

Nothing bad could ever happen to my mother, I was sure of it. She was faithful and good. What God would allow something to happen to my mother. Then you had to be a real miserable God, if you could make such mistakes. Impossible that the outcome would be anything other than good and so at an early age, I tried to exorcise my fears My father was called the next day by the insurance company, 'if they could send past an expert to assess the harm to a Ford Fairlane? My father almost fell off his chair and thought for a moment that the company was mistaken. 'Don't you know that you already have sent along someone ..' he started it and then it occurred to the fullest what possibly might have happened. 'Excuse me', he corrected himself, 'are you sure that no one has been sent passed?' 'Definitely,' the answer came, or words to that effect. My dad lip read the words to my brother. 'Hold on' my father said, into the black horn, 'the paper,' commanded my father, my brother handed it to him. 'Does this number mean anything to you,' asked my father and he read the number of the paper for.' Nothing,' said the voice on the other end. 'Thank you,' said my father, 'I'll soon be in touch with you.'

'Quickly,' said my father,' to the garage' and we went into a trot to the Opel and my father drove with a red contorted face behind the wheel towards the garage. The owner was on the phone but greeted my dad kindly as he walked out to meet him. 'Good afternoon,' my father said, 'where is the Ford' as he pointed to the empty parking lot.' Why, you have sold it a while ago,' answered the man, who gave my father a strange look. 'What do you mean I sold it,' my father said, without losing his temper. 'To a man who showed me the papers of the sale. He was the new owner and has transported it immediately.' 'Do you know where to?' 'No,' the owner,' said 'but the trailer had Egyptian number plates.' 'That says nothing, it is a neighboring country, but he may well have been on his way to Sudan.' 'Why Egypt or Sudan,' my father wanted to know.' Because wrecks are refurbished there and used for years as a taxi, the man said with a smile.' Thank you', my father said, and walked away.

Besides the car it snapped in him, he turned his hands, into claws and looked up, somewhere out there, where the sky should be and began, well, God .. damned I'll be ..... and he kept the rest to himself, fo a moment he had a desperate look in his eyes, he had let his defense let down and said 'God, why all the misery at once?'.

The Brooch

The days passed and one evening when we were at the table, my father told us that he was going to travel with my mother to the Netherlands, Amsterdam, to be exact. 'John Tidwel is coming to live with you, for a while during our absence,' he said, 'John is looking forward to it. He has spent too long without children.' My father smiled, but his eyes did not smile along. 'You have had the results of Malta,' asked my brother?' Yes, ', said my father and the outcome is not favorable. Your mother needs surgery as quickly as possible." Can that not be done in Malta' we wanted to know? 'Yes,' said my father,' but I've had enough of monkeys countries'. 'I have secured a list of hospitals that specialize in cancer research and I have seen that Malta is not on it. The best centre is located in the Netherlands, in Amsterdam and is called, 'van Leeuwenhoek hospital.' Even Americans travel to Amsterdam to be treated there.' I felt a sting, for just a moment of national pride.

'Are you going to be long', asked my sister? 'I do not know,' answered my father,' it depends on the hospital, but we'll keep in touch.' 'When are you leaving', I asked and I would have wanted to go with them, to wait and to give my mother courage or hold her hand. I knew that would not be possible. I suddenly had enough of this awful country that occasionally separated us and then cheated us again, the only nice Arabs were Arabs from other Arab countries. The Libyans respected only power and authority, and if you as a Christian Dog were just, being nice, that was a sign of weakness and they would hurt you, and where they could, cheat on you and if they got away with it, stone or kill you.

'Tomorrow', my father said, we will first f y to Malta and then a flight to Rome, and from there we will take one that goes directly to Amsterdam. The others felt reassured and saw it as a journey that my parents would make. No more than that. My mother would be all right after all, at the best hospital? But many years before I even would study, economics I felt unconsciously that there was such a thing as a Murphy's Law, if something can go wrong, it will go wrong. My father went to the office the next day to arrange things, and my mother prepared a travel bag and she laughed the problems away, 'if we need more,' she said,' we will buy it.' She still assumed that she would only be away for a short while.

She asked my sister to watch over my little sisters They were still really young. The oldest of the children was 5 and the youngest just 3. Now I ask myself at times what made my parents live in foreign countries with such young vulnerable children, I know the answer now, my father followed technical challenges and knew a lot about oil, he was born of Dutch parents in a colony himself. He did not know any better than living in Java and then once in a while going on leave to the Netherlands. My mother loved my father, she just breathed it out, she idolized the ground where he walked. She would follow him to any place, she could not live without him, and there was the answer in a nutshell.

When we were at home on the last night, there was a knock at the door and the clerk Achmed stood in front of it waiting when my father opened the door. He touched his heart, his lips and his forehead. My father asked him in, but he did not want to, he looked away, shy. His English was not good but very understandable. 'Friend of my master', he said, 'I have for you a letter and a parcel, I had to give it in your hands and walk out, so you can complete your goodbye.' He held out his hand and handed over a packet with an envelope. My father took it and Achmed's man bowed and was gone again. Outside a car door closed and a car drove off.' How does Achmed know that we are going,' asked my father as he closed the door?' I told him', my brother said. 'For what reason' my father wanted to know? 'Sorry', replied my brother and he turned a little red. 'This is our business', my father said with emphasis.

'Well, open the package,' my mother said, 'I wonder what's inside.' 'First, the letter,' said my father, and he unzipped the envelope and began to read. 'To my friend and benefactor, almost my father' it read, which would normally have sounded ridiculous but we understood the seriousness of the letter. I have a package for your lady who is going with you on a trip. I will not name the reason for the trip, as one must not invoke that which is evil. I offer a small gift of protection, I kissed it and held it against my heart. Ask your lady to wear it every day, please. *Allah Y Allah*, there is only one God and that is Allah and 147Mohammed is his prophet. I wish you all the best. Insha'Allah. If God wants it. Your friend, almost family, Achmed. My father's eyes were moist and my mother took the package and opened it. In a cotton bed lay jewelery, a brooch-like ornament. It was silver filigree, finely wrought and you could see the antiquity reflect from it. It was round in shape with fine silver wire that had melted under the hands of a skilled silversmith and had formed a black center, a black stone. A shield It would surely not be a piece of the kabala, from Mecca, I thought? In silver characters from right to left, gracefully calligraphed by a silversmith, a text was written in that black area, which we could read with our little knowledge of Arabic. *Allah Y Allah Ihmsha'alah.* It was beautiful, it was so I estimated, an amulet, an heirloom from his own family. Now, so many many years later I have it back in my possession and when I see it, I am thrown back in time and I sit next to her at the table and I see my mother, who took the brooch out of the box and pressed a kiss on it and held it against her heart. 'There is one God', she said, and he has many names. Insha' Allah.

With clean shoes

The day came when my mother and my father would leave us. A lot must have gone through my mother, she left her children behind in a distant country and did not know whether and how she would come back. It was such a brave sweet mother. A lot must have gone through my father as well, he left the only thing in his life of value to him, us and his work and went with the dream of his life to go and find a cure. In those days there were no fax machines, there were no cell phones and there was no facebook. When the door closed behind you, then the contact was broken. Libya and telephony were still in their infancy, and if something went wrong, terribly wrong, you were condemned to a telegram. So it was that in the morning a colleague of my father came along, who just came to say goodbye and take my parents to the airport. I remember that his name was Phil and of course he did something with technology. He was British, but in a way that you only see in nostalgic films. He radiated unimpeachable correctness.

My mom picked up her shoes and wanted to dust them off with a cloth, but Phil got up and held out his hand imperiously. He brushed them, rubbed them with some shoe cream and began to polish them as if his life depended on it. I saw it and although it seemed harmless, the message was clear to me, didn't my brother and sister see how every adult at the last minute wanted to do something nice for my mom. Each adult was concerned and knew more than we did.

Mr. Tidwel came in and he said in a jovial tone,' the prodigal son has found the door.' Everyone wanted to make small talk, but to me the coming parting of our ways hung very heavy in the air. That's how adults deal with problems, they don't lose sight of the facts, but they just mask their feelings, of their uncertainty. I had always been a good observer and I could read the uncertainty floating in the air. The hour of parting had come suddenly, much too fast and we hugged our parents, the farewell that was too short and was too business like. I hugged the woman I loved so much in a detached tough way. I wanted to hold her against me and wanted to protect her and take away her pain and I was willing to sacrifice myself for her. But it were just two kisses, one on each cheek. 'Will you be good', she asked and I nodded and she walked with my dad and Phil to the door, she waved from the car and we stood waving in a cloud of dust.

Next day, uncle John, because he had determined that mister was very formal, had received a message at his work from my parents and they had arrived safely. We simply accepted that. 'Today,' uncle John continued,' is a good day for a barbeque but I do need help,' and in those days he took our thoughts off our worries. He talked about dinosaurs and sediment layers and where the sand came from. Sand was just sediment, I had never thought about that. 'But' he said, pointing at me,' my favorite nephew knows all about that, he's been on one of my stone tapping expeditions." He was one of my best assistants so far' and he gloated at that.

In the evening after the meal he would read from his own Bible a verse or two. No brimstone or hell and damnation but just in a normal tone of voice. It was a bound Bible and I remember, now, years later, that it had the words,' the King James version' written on the side. Later, many years later, I would always also find a king James bible in whichever American hotel room, waiting for the guest who needed to illuminate himself with a reading. He was funny but serious and he would have been a good father. He had been brought up in an orphanage, and he said it was important to show solidarity and that daily food was always welcome. That a prayer could not hurt anyone and that there were people who worried every day about where the next meal would come from. Gratitude, there was no food discarded.

My brother went to school and I went to mine and my sister took care of the kids and uncle John was working a few hours a day at the office and wrote for the rest many reports on the living room table. The days shuffled past. He came from Texas and asked if we knew the song, ***the Yellow Rose of Texas***? Within the month, that my parent's absence lasted, we learned many cowboy songs and we had become convinced that Texas, the lone star state, was the best place on earth. When he said that, he just tapped on his boots, 'handmade in Texas,' he laughed, touching the lone star on the side. 'After a few years they grow to your feet.' 'Tomorrow there is no cooking', said uncle John one day,' I've got some friends coming over and we are going to enjoy it'. Indeed a day later in the afternoon, two cars drew up and there were a group of Texans who unfolded a bunch of tables and turned them into a kind of buffet.

'This', said uncle John, 'I've missed, good Mexican food and some spare ribs.' It was asking much for someone who had never been father to five children to be responsible all the time all of the sudden and of course uncle John had his own friends and they had stopped by. They did not enter my father's house except to go to the toilet or to get something from the kitchen. Yes, after some time, every second song was the *Yellow Rose of Texas, the streets of Laredo or the Navajo trail.* The Streets of Laredo was an impressive song for my brother and me, it was about a young gunslinger who lay dying where he had been shot, with a chorus filled with melancholy and knowledge: **for I am a young cowboy and I know I've done wrong.** My brother who had always read cowboy books, loved it, heraldry and young unnecessary death, resulting from machismo, it spoke very much to his imagination.

The days turned into weeks and I realized that it was not all as good as the others who were lulled to sleep, might have assumed. Uncle John now took his vacation. He did that in half days, he worked in the office and then came home early. My youngest sisters began to speak English, "mornin'uncle John", it sounded with little voices that unmistakably spoke with a Texan accent. When the news came that my parents would come home, uncle John had to go to the desert to a concession where there were some problems, an outpost concession, near where the foundation had been flown in, on my only stay in the desert. He gave my brother and my sister a number and said, 'if there was anything at all,' to call this number, 'I just need to be present,' he said,' but I'll be back within a few days.'

It was the company's number. 'Gee,' I said,' but uncle John, tomorrow my parents will come home.' 'Give them my regards,' he said, 'I will come past next week,' unfortunately that was not to be, the hand of hatred had slowly awakened and was waiting for Uncle John and his colleagues, 'Listen to your brother and sister,' he said, to me and walked to the van of the company, waved and disappeared forever from our lives. God rest his soul. The man who had so unselfishly taken care of the children of his friend and colleague would never see Texas again and would never sing about Yellow roses anymore. The hand made sure of that, the hand that squeezed every Christian dog to pulp.

cowboy boots

We were ecstatic when the car of Phil's came driving up the parking lot with my parents in it. My mother was the only one that caught my eye, she looked tired and she had different color hair. My father and Phil took some bags out of his car and we went to sit down at the big table. I probably spoke out of turn, but I wanted to be the first to say something.' I am so glad to see you again,' I said, and she looked at me with a sweet tired smile, 'Maantje', she said and smiled. it was her pet name for me and I knew she was really happy. It was as if we, alone, just sat at the table and looked at each other. Phil pulled up his chair and broke the magic moment. 'I am also glad that I'm back', she said, 'but I am very tired, I'm going to rest' and Dad will tell us what has happened. She drank some water and shied away with her left hand, when the kids came running to embrace her, 'not on that side,' she said, and kissed the girls diligently.' I really need to rest,' Dad will be back soon and he'll explain it all'. They vanished together into the bedroom and I understood that my mother needed help to undress. 'So', Phil, started, 'you all still had a bit of a good time with Uncle John' He has talked our ears from our head in the office, about his new nephews and nieces. I had a little chuckle. 'You can laugh about it,' Phil said, 'we went crazy.' 'Next time I'm your uncle,' he went on, we need to share the time on the nephews and nieces a bit, you know'. 'Will there be a next time', I asked? Was there something wrong with my brother and sister, did they not hear those things? 'Your father will tell you, but I suppose so, occasionally anyway and he kept his mouth shut wisely. My father sat down and looked around and he looked very tired. Pragmatist that he was, he told in a few sentences what the state of affairs was. 'The result was not positive, you know that', my father said, 'which was why we went away.' The tests were done again because the van Leeuwenhoek hospital has its own laboratory and wanted to check their own results. Which were negative as well. Your mother had surgery, she had some metastases, her lymph nodes are also removed' Short, always short, with not a word too much. I probably looked uncomprehendingly. My father pointed under his armpit,' 153here, he said, are your lymphe glands.' 'Oh,' I said. 'She has poor use of her left arm as a result, but that will improve'.

'The problem is solved now,' I asked? He looked at me and then answered, 'there will be checks every few months and treatment.' My father had answered a different question than the one I had asked.

He had eluded me. 'How's mum,' I asked, louder than I wanted? 'She has radioactive treatment,' he replied, 'a cobalt treatment, therefore Mom will wear a wig for a while.' 'I will occasionally go back and forth with her'. He knew what I was afraid of and did not want to comment.' Thank you', I said, 'it is clear to me'. My father had nothing but pain in his eyes, I could read him like a book and he could read me. At that moment the phone rang and my dad took the handset. 'Yes,' he said, 'he is still with me' My father listened and turned red, then there was a click that we even heard from where we sat, my father looked with disbelief at the handset. 'Phil, we cannot lose any time,' he said,' code red; an intervention force is being flown in to concession 52 via Wheelus airbase.' In about half an hour we will have a briefing with the big boss at headquarters, along with people from Red Adair.' 'You won't go to school tomorrow,' he told me and my brother, 'you stay here and look after the house.' He ran away with big steps and Phil ran after him, a bit later the car tires spun dirt into our yard and sped away. 'There is something very wrong,' my brother said. 'That is why,' said my brother, 'an intervention force has been flown in!' I had heard only words that were incoherent to me. A code that was red and something about an intervention force. It had no meaning to me. 'What is an intervention force', I asked my brother who apparently was better informed. 'Oil,' taught my brother, 'is important to the American economy. America will not allow its industry to suffer from an interruption in oil supply.' 'Yes,' I said? 'On several American Bases 'troops are stationed who have a specific task, therefore they are called a task force. It is an open secret that America has a stand by intervention or task force spread around the Mediterranean area. An intervention force of 100,000 men' 'That force, will protect the American oil interests. Anyway, they can have access within a few hours to 100,000 men, but here they might fly in only 2000 men.' Is that all right with Libya,' I asked? 'If the concessions are leased by American companies, it is an American interest'. 'The force solves the problem and there after it is ironed out politically where needed'

'Okay,' I said, 'that it is clear to me,' I had never heard my brother say so many sensible things in succession. 'Who is Red Adair, because that's who Dad and Phil are going to talk to?' 'No', my brother said, 'not Red Adair, but people of Red Adair.' ' Who cares,' I said, 'who is that?' 'That is a Texan who has a group of people, trained to extinguish oil wells.' 'Is that so difficult then,' I wondered? 'Almost impossible,' replied my brother, who was in a technical college. 'Water cannot be used that will only dilute the oil. 'Hey it's crude, crude oil.' 'Okay,' I said, how do Red or the people that work for him, extinguish a burning well?' 'He is an blowout expert', knew my brother, 'he used to be an explosives man in the army and he crawls in a special suit to the mouth of the oil well and throws a bomb in it . 'Hey', I said? My mouth fell open.' Oh, yeah', continued my brother, 'fire requires oxygen if you throw a bomb into the furnace, such as in any burning source, then the explosion causes a vacuum and then the fire is out'. 'It is not like smoldering wood, it's oil, right?' 'Gosh, they had managed to teach my brother something in that college, it flashed through me. 'Is that not terribly dangerous,' I wanted to know?' My brother looked at me like I was insane. 'You bet,' he said, really, extremely dangerous. If you work for a while in the group of Red Adair then you are rich beyond imagination, on the other hand nobody wants to insure you.' I got the picture. Suddenly I saw the connection.

'Get this', I said this is very serious, uncle John had to be present at something, a concession, remember what number?" No,' my brother replied,' he did not say, however, he did say it was close to the new foundation, an outpost or something.' 'I saw it, the Romney shed and all before me, which had been a canteen to me, the buildings and the runway. The shelters and the control room next to the guard post. There were guards, I thought, fortunately, they were not unprotected. 'That', I said slowly, 'is concession 52.' 'I know it,' I said. There is something going on there that the guards could not handle, that is why the intervention force is flying in, something serious.' 'There's a fire or fire hazard, otherwise there would not be a team of Red Adair oil well fire fi ghters ready in the main office". No,' my brother said, 'you're almost right'. 'The Red Adair people need to consult with the engineers, the technicians.' 'I guess I know what the orders are,' I said, 'the intervention force clears everything and everyone that should not be there.' 'If wells are burning , the Red Adair people extinguish those fires.' 'Yes,' said my brother and the technicians have to give a shut down to a burning refinery with hydrogen storage next to it, which is highly explosive, the plant must be shut down or you'll have have different spreads of fire piped to other concessions. That is where Dad comes in with Phil and his group of people, I'm sure. John is already there,' My sister, mingled in now and said, 'it makes no sense to look at the back of an embroidery.'

The taxi stopped two days and two nights later in front our house and my father and Philip got out. They were hollow-eyed and smelled of fire and smoke, they stumbled more than they walked. I had never seen my father with stubble and grime. He spoke whimpering, 'go away, go to your room, I just want to talk to your mother.' My mother saw him coming and got up, 'come here boy,' she said comfortingly and my dad broke. After long sobs, he managed to bring out, 'they're all dead'. 'Boy sshhttt,' said my mother, and she stroked his cheek and now Phil started, gently at first and then uncontrollably, shaking and sobbing.' Get some water,' she shouted at us and it did not matter to my father anymore, he had to tell the story and the story was a nightmare.

Among the guards had been extremists, who first killed the guards who were proAmerican ritually, as if they were goats. ' Then they went to the canteen' my father said and mutilated and slaughtered the whites'. He could not talk anymore and hid his head in his hands. Phil said,' no', he started again, it just did not pass his lips, no one has a head". Oh, my God, I thought, how far does evil reach?' 'Then they burned the bodies.' We know that,' Phil said, 'from the Arab that had f ed into the desert, the Task Force found him.' 'Then they went inside the control room and murdered everyone and pushed buttons until a pressure line blew up and they emptied their guns on the equipment, while they shouted *Alluh Akbar*. It has been burning for days We took care of the shutdown,' he looked frantically around himself 'and the men of Red are now working'.

'I do not want to sleep,' moaned Phil, suddenly, 'I can never sleep again'. We all stood transfixed so many horrors that we heard within a few seconds.' And John', my mother asked? 'I recognized him by his boots,' my father said who again seemed to get control himself. I saw him, cheerfully singing the Yellow Rose and glorifying his boots tapping the lone Star with his finger. 'There is nothing left of him to return to Texas.

Suddenly my father got up with a jerk and walked to the back door and looked out, he was really on his last legs. 'I thought I saw him' he said.' Come on John,' *adoeh*, come on in man,' and I knew what he was doing, he was born in Indonesia. He invited uncle John in. 'Come home boy'. Don't you see him standing there, he asked despairingly over his shoulder? 'Call the doctor,' my mother said to my brother. My father told my sister to get flour, 'we must have flour all over the floor, I want to see his steps. Come on boy the best seat is for you' and he walked out as if he was going to meet someone. There he stood, and he looked up, the moon was not full yet, but I felt what he was going to do and the hairs stood on end on my arms and legs. He stretched out his arms, and there was a melancholy cry to the clouds and the moon and my father was howling his soul out and collapsed.

Tribal understanding

Life would not never be the same for us again. New people would be contracted, engineers and geologists and everyone and everything that was needed to get oil out of the ground. The company would pay them princely wages and they would come in good spirits, and with an open heart, the new Westerners would plan to get on well with the host country. Eventually experiences would cause them to harden and to be what we had become. People who looked over their shoulder when they heard steps and distrust people in advance, they would always estimate risks in whatever situation. Their attitude would feed the evil that haunts Libya and people would be talking about all of us as the *white Satani*, the devils, the heretics, the arrogant Christian dogs. Imams would seize the illiteracy of their flock to offer from the Koran texts, filtered to their own limited insights that would lead to hatred and justify hatred and incite intolerance. While the Koran is a beautiful book, a revelation of a man, a prophet who gave insights, to offer humanity a philosophical hold on Divine manner, to improve a world, that very same message has been abused out of context and raped and used for their own purposes. The Prophet Muhammad, like Jesus, was a world improver, a voice from the wilderness. A voice that tried to share with humanity a way of life, to be closer to the creator. Jesus, the man of love, would have been abhorred by popes who would order crusades in his name and Muhammad cannot have meant that one human being should ritually slaughter the other like a goat, in the name of Allah. Envy, poverty or political objectives are covered with a layer of Religion and many avid texts, taken out of context to justify our destruction. We, the Westerners were to be the scapegoats of Libyan Imams. Without being heard, we were the Jews in Nazi Germany, we were persecuted for no reason and we had no rights, formally we did, but we could not practice them and crystal night fell whenever possible, hunting us and damaging us. Not so visible, as the smashed windows in Germany, but as the evil that grew and roamed the hearts of those living in backward areas like Libya, which was feudally exploited by its own leaders and manipulated by imams. We were not put in concentration camps, but locked ourselves in concentration like complexes behind barbed wire in order to be less vulnerable and to be safe.

The hatred of the pavement, shouted up to us, wherever we went, we felt it every day and I believed it to be increasing in intensity daily. Something had been set in motion, something negative that was increasingly directed against us. As a rowing boat that first begins to oscillate at a given movement in time, increasing in momentum before turning over. We lived on a powder keg. The Eta, the IRA, the Taliban, the former Yugoslavia, the Basque Country, Catalonia, Northern Ireland and Quebec, are all examples of separatist tribal connections that mask pursued political goals. Thus, the Libyan masses were dangerous, there was no defined political objective that limited attacks and then every action against the outsiders becomes a victory.

After the senseless death of uncle John and his colleagues I understood him better. He had once before, in the days of the petrified forest, given explanations to me about Mo's and tribalism. In Libya at the invitation of its Government itself, a foreign tribe had settled down. The root name of that tribe was: Americans and in that tribe were subdivisions, substrains. The military and the Texans from the lone star state. The all interconnecting link was one of oil people and technicians and their protectors. The Libyan government had also allowed, against monstrous amounts of dollars, an airbase lease contract. The undeveloped Libyans confused all our tribal ties alike. We were white, so we were American in their eyes. An American oilman or military were unified, and when they saw a white man, he would be a non Muslims, then you were immediately placed in the tribe of the Christian dogs. The undeveloped mind, driven by hate and envy, does not distinguish between Americans and Westerners. Those scary spirits make use of fallacies, all Americans are Westerners so all Westerners are Americans and every one is a Christian dog.

It was not the same and in came weeks with meetings and memorial services, and three weeks later what had happened slowly ebbed away, the daily routine had won from the grief. But no one was the same anymore, we had become more cynical. At school, the children of the murdered oil men were missing, they had returned with their mother and a good pension to civilization. There was even a small memorial service at school. That same school which had held a Libyan week that year as part of the brotherhood week. There was only one tribe that had the intention to live in peace and that was our tribe and the other tribe gave rise to the evil that only wanted to destroy us. We did not belong to their tribal area. The satirical song had been played then over the intercom every day, it conveyed now a very different meaning: ***all the black folks hate the white folks..and the white folks hate the black folks*** it was now seen more than ever as truth stripped of sarcasm.

Time ticked by and my mother visited twice the van Leeuwenhoek hospital with my dad, but that was for a short stay and then she was declared clean. The joy was great in our house, but I told you, we had changed. I kept fearful doubts, which I obviously did not utter, because you must not call on misfortune, as Achmed had taught me, and unfortunately my cynicism became true a few years later. One evening we were sitting at the table and my father said, I've had a very interesting offer. We all listened closely.

'An offer to extend my contract with four years and then be appointed auditor of the company'. It remained silent. 'What do you want,'asked my mother? I hate this country, my father said, 'simply hate it'.. 'Will we go back to the Netherlands,' I asked? 'No, I don't think so, because we no longer fit in their way of life'. I understood that, we had always lived in different oil-producing countries every 4 or 5 years. You get a different perspective because of it. Not necessarily through better glasses, just another way of looking at things. This creates a different perspective. 'Gosh', my mother said, 'why don't we go to Texas.' You'll still have the racial problem', said my father. I understood him, America had just risen above the segregation laws. It would be a long time before a balance would come about, a real equality.

'There are only two countries', said my father, 'that qualify in my opinion. Australia or Canada. South Africa, I think is far too dangerous,' I want to get away from Africa anyway.' There was no google in those days, in fact there was no internet at all. It meant little to us. We knew nothing of the two options. Vague things like the kangaroos in Australia or the Eskimos in Canada. 'I got a good offer from Alberta Canada,' he continued,' but in the Brisbane area in Australia a great oil reserve is waiting for me. Both are commonwealth countries, they are part of the British Commonwealth. In both countries, we can speak English'. 'What is the safest country,' asked my sister. 'Canada', my father said. 'You can just wait for the Asians to make a move again and then Australia stands no chance.' I did have an image about that, the Japanese had also overrun Indonesia, his native country and occupied it in the last war.

'Furthermore, it is there just as hot as here". Oh,' my mother said suddenly with sparkling eyes, the film ***Oh, Rosemary I love you,*** was that not shot in Canada?' 'That was a great movie, I loved it, the snow and the mountains and the royal mounted police who always find their man'. Yes, my father said, and there is a strict admission policy, other tribes are not so fast in and it lies under the protective umbrella of America. I still have half a year's time, ending my contract, but I'll take it into consideration'. That night I dreamed about polar bears and Eskimo huts. Thus fate, on the basis of a film that my mother had seen would lead us to Canada, but prematurely. Because fate made us flee to save our mortal selves. The hand of evil did not only search around anymore, the hand had become a fist and in June 1967 in the war that followed, it crushed and shattered, burnt, raped and killed everything that was not Arabic. We fled, leaving our possessions and memories and dead behind.

Rest in peace uncle John

God Bless you all!

San Daniel 2014

About the Author

San Daniel is an Andalusian vintner who left the academic life behind years ago. He now lives in Southern Spain. He walked into a Spanish village and never left it again. The village recognized him as a prodigal son and locked him in her arms in a warm and lasting embrace. San Daniel broke with his former life and became happy and became a vintner and writer. His heart has become Andalucian!